✦ ✦ ✦ ✦ ✦ ✦ ✦ ✦ ✦ ✦ ✦

Words of Praise for

Seven Secrets
to Raising a Happy
and Healthy Child

"Joyce presents an intriguing and novel exploration of parenting, filled with a mother's love and common sense, as well as an examination of Ayurvedic principles. Parenting is always automatically a mind/body laboratory, and by being explicit and thoughtful about mind/body principles, we can greatly enhance the process. Accordingly, this book enormously expands on what might seem obvious, offering both concrete suggestions for what to do, as well as presenting challenging concepts for why to do them. The wisdom of the ages and the wisdom of a child— a perfect marriage for a book."

— **Daniel Einhorn, M.D., F.A.C.E.**

✦ ✦ ✦ ✦ ✦ ✦ ✦ ✦ ✦ ✦ ✦

+ + + + + + + + + + +

The Seven Secrets

+ The first secret is caring for the baby in the womb from the moment of conception.

+ The second secret is learning to identify the baby's mind/body type—or *dosha*—by observing his or her eating and sleeping patterns, sensitivity to light and noise, and interaction with others.

+ The third secret is learning to center yourself while calming and soothing your baby.

+ The fourth secret is a daily body massage for the baby, which improves sleep patterns, muscle tone, digestion, and resistance to disease.

+ The fifth secret is to employ simple yoga and breathing techniques with your baby, which improves alertness and coordination; and regulates hunger, thirst, sleep, and digestion.

+ The sixth secret is making the proper nutrition choices that best serve individual body types.

+ The seventh secret is using rest, massage, tonics, and diet to ease childbirth, avoid postpartum depression, and nurture your baby and yourself.

+ + + + + + + + + + +

✦ ✦ ✦ ✦ ✦ ✦ ✦ ✦ ✦ ✦ ✦

SEVEN SECRETS

to Raising a Happy
and Healthy Child

✦ ✦ ✦ ✦ ✦ ✦ ✦ ✦ ✦ ✦ ✦

+ + + + + + + + + + +

SEVEN SECRETS

to Raising a Happy and Healthy Child

+ + + + + + + + + + +

The Ayurvedic Approach to Parenting

+ + + + + + + + + + +

Joyce Golden Seyburn

Hay House, Inc.
Carlsbad, California • Sydney, Australia
Canada • Hong Kong • United Kingdom

Published and distributed in the United States by: Hay House, Inc., P.O. Box
5100, Carlsbad, CA 92018-5100 • *Phone:* (760) 431-7695 or (800) 654-5126
Fax: (760) 431-6948 or (800) 650-5115 • www.hayhouse.com • *Published and
distributed in Australia by:* Hay House Australia Pty Ltd, 18/36 Ralph St.,
Alexandria NSW 2015 • *Phone:* 612-9669-4299 • Fax: 612-9669-4144 • *e-mail:*
info@hayhouse.com.au • *Published and Distributed in the United Kingdom by:*
Hay House UK, Ltd. • Unit 202, Canalot Studios • 222 Kensal Rd., London
W10 5BN • *Phone:* 020-8962-1230 • *Fax:* 020-8962-1239 • *Distributed in
Canada by:* Raincoast • 9050 Shaughnessy St., Vancouver, B.C. V6P 6E5 • *Phone:*
(604) 323-7100 • *Fax:* (604) 323-2600

Editorial supervision: Jill Kramer • *Design:* Jenn Ramsey • *Illustrations:* Laurie Meier

This book was originally published by The Berkley Publishing Group in
March 1998: ISBN: 0425-16166-8

Library of Congress Cataloging-in-Publication Data

Seyburn, Joyce Golden.
  Seven secrets to raising a happy and healthy child : the ayurvedic approach
to parenting / Joyce Golden Seyburn.
     p. cm.
Includes bibliographical references and index.
  ISBN 1-40190-109-3 (Tradepaper)
  1.   Pregnancy—Popular works. 2.   Infants—Care—Popular works.
3. Medicine, Ayurvedic. I. Title.
  RJ61 .S4465 2003
  649'.122—dc21
                    2002153972

                ISBN 1-4019-0109-3

         06 05 04 03   4 3 2 1
         1st printing, March 2003

              Printed in Canada

CONTENTS

+ + + + + + + + + + +

Editor's Note: *To avoid awkward he/she construction, the feminine
pronoun has been used predominantly throughout this book.*

✦ ✦ ✦ ✦ ✦ ✦ ✦ ✦

FOREWORD

✦ ✦ ✦ ✦ ✦ ✦ ✦ ✦

When Joyce asked me to contribute the Foreword for this book, I agreed because of my interest in mind/body medicine. I became interested in this approach to medicine approximately seven years ago when I opened my women's health center. From several of my patients who are interested in a holistic approach to their health issues, I have learned how wonderful the combination of Western and Eastern medicine can be in treating a number of health problems. Several recent articles have discussed the scientific connection between mind and body, especially when dealing with stress. Certain disease states are treated more appropriately by Western medicine, and some more appropriately by Eastern approaches.

I have enjoyed knowing Joyce for the past seven years as an informed patient. She really does lead her life in the manner she discusses in her book.

As a board-certified obstetrician/gynecologist, I found this book to be an eye-opener. What was new to me was the whole concept of each woman nurturing her pregnancy in a mind/body fashion, although it really does make a lot of sense. Pregnancy is a unique and wonderful time in a woman's life; knowing the seven secrets described in this book can enhance this already special time. The seven secrets will encourage each woman to look at herself emotionally and spiritually and prepare for a journey that she may never be able to experience again. They give women the tools to approach their pregnancy in a holistic and spiritual way. Women nurturing their pregnancy will automatically feel a special bond with their infants if they mentally begin to think of their pregnancy in a mind/body fashion.

Many women are accustomed to taking care of someone else and not nurturing themselves. Women are really remarkable human beings because they usually care for themselves last. By reading this book and embracing its mind/body practices, I hope that you'll begin to accept your pregnancy as a priority, and feel good about being pregnant! Your health and well-being and your baby's health and well-being are equally important. This is the time to begin showing your baby just how much you care for him or her and to embark on a beautiful and well-deserved childbirth journey. Raising a child is a commitment you make for life. Reading and enjoying *Seven Secrets to Raising a Happy and Healthy Child* will help you make this commitment more special. This information will be helpful not only during pregnancy, but after birth as well. Raising a child with exposure to mind/body techniques will help in the child's approach to wellness and the handling of disease.

I truly enjoyed reading this book and will recommend it to my own patients.

— **Rosalyn Baxter-Jones, M.D.,** President and CEO, Women's Health Pavilion, San Diego

✦✦✦   ✦✦✦

ACKNOWLEDGMENTS

Just as a tapestry is woven with many strands of yarn, so was my book woven together with many eyes to scrutinize, hands to shuffle the pages, and hearts to encourage me. Thank you, one and all, from the bottom of my heart.

My heartfelt thanks go out to my dear friends Lee Carroll and Jan Tober. I thank my Putnam editor, Denise Silvestro, whose probing eye helped me expand my concepts; my picky local editor and friend Mo Raphael; my manuscript typist, Penny Monroe; my computer consultant, Angelo Riveria, who helped me through many a traumatic moment; Hay House editor Jill Kramer, a caring, constructive companion on the road to reprinting; and my talented artist/illustrator, Laurie Meier, for her diligence.

Thanks to Denise McGregor, my good friend and fellow writer, who helped keep me on my path to publication with her dramatic diligence.

I want to thank all the wonderful women who gave me their stories; The Chopra Center for my first introduction to Ayurveda; Veera Sanjana for her wonderful Ayurvedic meals and nutritional counseling; and Bruce Seyburn for his timely support.

Most of all, I want to thank my children Marc, Alisa, and Shelby, for listening to my mind/body recommendations and trying them out; Ryan, who, although he lived abroad during my time at the computer, gave me spiritual encouragement over the wire; and Angie, who believed in me enough to give me space to finish my book. I'd also like to thank my sisters and mother, who taught me unconditional love.

Thank you, one and all!

+++   +++

INTRODUCTION

"Healthy people live neither in the past
nor in the future. They live in the present,
in the Now, which gives the Now a flavor of
eternity because no shadows fall across it."

— Deepak Chopra

Seven Secrets to Raising a Happy and Healthy Child is a practical guide to helping you understand your child's constitution (mind/body type) so that you can be confident about maintaining his or her optimum health. You'll learn why *your* child is a light sleeper and why your friend's child is a sound sleeper. You'll learn why *your* baby gets diaper rash so easily, while your neighbor's child never gets a rash. You'll learn why some children can't stand still—and how they can be quieted with a rhythm, not a struggle. If your child is sluggish, you'll learn that you can increase vitality through spices and activities. I'm going to help you understand how simple it is to decipher your children's unique constitutional profile so that you can keep them in optimum health.

The most complete health system I've found is an Indian health system more than 5,000 years old called *Ayurveda*, which means "the science of life." Ayurveda works because it gives a framework for looking at the individual in terms of his or her unique construction. A person's constitution consists of a physical, an emotional, and a psychological body that must stay in harmony in order to remain healthy. Ayurveda provides specific guidelines and practices that can assist you in keeping that balance in yourself and in your baby.

In this book, I offer simple practices that you can perform from prebirth through childhood. I believe that once these mind/body practices are established in early childhood, they'll be naturally integrated into your children's lives as they grow into adulthood.

This is all about assisting your child on the balance beam of health. Babies depend on their parents to take care of their needs. They know when they're uncomfortable— they may cry, get sick, throw a tantrum, or act taciturn— but they don't know what's wrong or what will ease their discomfort. As parents, it's our job to figure out what our children need to keep them in optimal health. We need to take care of them and teach them to take care of themselves. As they grow, they'll be accustomed to the balancing practices and procedures you've taught them. They'll be more aware when they're out of balance, and will know how to restore this sense of harmony.

Because we teach our children best through example, I've designed this book to help you know *yourself,* so in turn you'll know and understand your child.

+++

"The world has a beginning
And this beginning could be called
the mother of the world.
When you have known the mother
Go on to know the child,
After you have known the child
Go back to holding fast to the mother,
And to the end of days you will not
meet with danger."

— Lao Tzu

According to Ayurveda, a balanced mind and body is the first step toward a long, healthy, and happy life. There is no room for disease in the body when the mind is totally aware of any uncomfortable feelings, because it will naturally seek to bring everything back in balance. The mind is very powerful, and it exerts a tremendous amount of influence on the body. When the mind is aware of an imbalance, it makes the body correct itself. Conversely, if the mind is troubled, this will be manifested physically in the form of illness, pain, or discomfort. Thus, the goal of the Ayurvedic health-care system is to maintain mind/body balance and help us become more aware of our bodies and ourselves so that we can recognize imbalance and correct it.

The fundamental principle behind Ayurveda is similar to that of a symphony. All the sections of the orchestra that play in our mind/body symphony must be in harmony in order for the melody to resonate. However, if even one instrument is off-key, the melody will be discordant.

In our society, we've recently begun to stress the idea of balance within many disciplines. Magazines are constantly promoting one diet or another for its ability to

balance our weight. Workout studios and gyms are promoting "balanced" exercise programs. And psychologists
always seem to be talking about "mental imbalances" and
how to correct them with therapy and/or drugs. However,
although balance is the goal, the problem is that these
approaches are fragmented. Nowhere are we shown a fundamental thread to weave all these disparate pieces of our
lives together. The practice of Ayurveda is precisely about
attaining this larger balance in our lives.

Ayurveda is about being *conscious* of the delicate balance within. Perhaps there's a slight biochemical imbalance in your body that you're not aware of. Perhaps your
body doesn't feel like it's at its peak performance level. At
first it's a small thing, and you ignore it, but it persists.
Rest assured that such a matter can get out of hand if you
don't take a look at what's amiss in your system. Imagine
a dancer moving fluidly, at one with the music. If that
dancer twisted her ankle and continued to dance on it,
her movements would be slightly uncoordinated and
clumsy. Perhaps she'd put more weight on the unsprained
ankle. Soon her body would tilt toward the good ankle,
and her shoulder would turn slightly downward. She'd be
off balance. There would cease to be fluidity in her movements. She might eventually fall.

Mind over matter is not always the appropriate way to
handle an imbalance. Ayurveda teaches us *mindfulness*. It
encourages us to pay attention to our small aches and
pains, and to not discount or deny them. Ayurveda teaches us to be attentive to our symptoms, to understand what
they mean, and to take appropriate action.

A friend of mine awoke one morning with a stiff neck
and shoulder. She tried stretching it out, then put a muscle-
relaxing cream on it, but the pain and discomfort continued.

Every day she took something to mask the pain and continued to tell herself that she must have slept on her shoulder "funny." After three months of nagging pain, it wasn't "funny" anymore. She finally went to her doctor and he took an x-ray, which showed a tiny grain of something in her shoulder, but instead of exploring it further, to come up with the cause, the doctor sent her to a physical therapist who worked on her three times a week for eight months. She still had no relief. Finally, the doctor acquiesced to additional testing and had my friend take an MRI. It revealed that she had a bone spur on her shoulder, which was pressing on a nerve and interfering with her movement. By this time, her movement was restricted to the point that she couldn't raise her arm above her waistline without excruciating pain. An operation was recommended, and it took place the following week.

Obviously my friend learned about her body the hard way. In retrospect, we know that the signals her body was giving could have been dealt with proactively, and she could have avoided the operation. Bone spurs occur from lack of calcium in the body (not, as commonly assumed, from too much calcium). Had she increased her calcium intake by eating more leafy green vegetables and adding more dairy foods to her diet, she might have avoided the months of severe pain by rebalancing her body before the bone spur had time to grow.

Ayurveda weaves us back into balance. All we have to do is pay attention to the basics, listen to our bodies, then respond productively by using Ayurveda's age old, tried-and-true solutions. These solutions come in the form of diet, touch and/or breathing, moving, or silent meditative practice.

As a former kindergarten teacher, I remember the striking contrasts between the happy, healthy, energetic children and the sullen, sickly, and unenergetic kids in my classes. I used to contemplate the reasons for the differences, and although there are no simple answers, one very evident characteristic separated the two groups of children. The sullen, sickly, unenergetic kids were usually those whose families were dysfunctional. The happy, seemingly healthy, and energetic children were from more stable home environments. I concluded at the time that the sullen group was out of balance in one or more facets of their lives. The happy group seemed to have a more balanced life. (This is a generality.)

I started to wonder when the imbalances actually started. Do babies come into this world balanced? If so, how can we preserve their precious balance? Over the years I've asked myself these questions again and again.

I carefully watched my three children go from babyhood to adult life, doing what I could to keep that inner spark of health alive. I intuitively knew this was the key to a healthy, happy life. I had no knowledge of Ayurveda or of mind/body practices at the time. Thankfully, my children—now 22, 25, and 28—grew up happy and healthy.

Unfortunately, no instruction manuals come with babies. And even though there are hundreds of child-care books on the market in this country, most parents still depend on their mothers or grandmothers to show them what to do and how to do it. There are thousands of cultures on this planet, and each culture handles labor and birth practices a little differently. Many practices are ritualized procedures that seem to get the mother and baby off to a good start. But few other than Ayuveda tell us how to *maintain* that optimum healthy condition.

I've incorporated many of the recommendations from Ayurveda into this book. I believe I have westernized Ayurveda by interlacing it with an occasional principle from another culture and by selecting practices from yoga and other systems that have the greatest application to pregnancy and early childhood.

Seven Secrets to Raising a Happy and Healthy Child explains how we're all alike and how we differ from each other. It explains balance, and how this quality is the most vital ingredient for a healthy life. The practices in this book are actually preventive health routines. Knowing your own and your baby's mind/body type is the first step. This dictates the degree and direction of all further steps needed to maintain or restore balance.

Wisdom has no expiration date, and this ancient wisdom from India has been proven true for thousands of years. Western medicine is only a few hundred years old and is based on technology, not nature's own system of balance and rebalance. I believe that it's entirely appropriate for Eastern and Western medicine to be brought together, especially when our children stand to benefit.

How This Book Came About

The event that led me to write this book took place during my experience of the birth of my first grandbaby, Shelby. I was invited to be in the birthing room with my son Marc and daughter-in-law, Alisa. The room was rather small for the assemblage of people who gathered around Alisa. Her mother and my son flanked her sides and assisted her with breathing. I found a small corner on the upper side of her bed where I could stand next to her heartbeat monitor. Extending my arms over and above Alisa's abdomen, I began feeling the energy of a new life readying to emerge. As the vibrating Shelby pushed out of the womb, I felt a tremendous surge of energy. The miracle of birth, witnessed by my eyes and hands, gave me an overwhelming feeling of *bliss*.

What is bliss? Imagine yourself on a beach watching one wave and then another crash onto the shoreline. Each wave takes you deeper into the moment. You look up, and as you do, you see the expansive ocean and get an overwhelming "ah-ha!" feeling. That feeling is bliss. I'd reached bliss other times in my life—during my children's births and the adoption of my daughter—but Shelby's birth opened me up completely to it.

I began to ponder the pure innocence of babies coming into the world, full of love to give. Again questions surfaced: What happens to that innocence and purity? What happens to the "ah-ha!" feeling of wonder children seem to have? What changes it? How can we preserve it? How can we help to keep it alive and thriving? After all, children are our most precious gift. We're entrusted with them for a very short time in comparison to their life span. We help set the foundation on which they'll build their lives. Let us give them all the tools they need to keep their lives balanced and their bodies healthy.

I know that adults who maintain that spark tend to stay more youthful and healthy than those who lose it. My father, for example, had a real zest for life. He was diagnosed with cancer and was told by his doctors at the Mayo Clinic that he had only six months to live. He lived for another 13 years—and was written up in a medical journal because no one before him had lived that long with Hodgkin's disease (a cancer of the lymph glands).

His "zest for life" was the reason the doctors gave for his remission. He lived his life in a state of bliss, and that kept him healthy.

+ + +

"One whose physiology is in balance and whose body, mind, and senses remain full of Bliss is called a healthy person."

— Shushruta Samhita

In our culture, bliss has a frivolous connotation. In the ancient practice of Ayurveda, bliss has a joyful, profound meaning; it's synonymous with total health and balance. Ayurveda promotes health in that it aims to return us to that sense of bliss and balance we were born with. I hope that this book, which is written from my heart, will help you, as parents, learn how you can *maintain* that purest bliss and balance your baby came into the world with.

That spark, that crystallized glow we see in the eyes of children, that state of joy and wonder—that's bliss. I see it in my granddaughter Shelby's eyes. On a recent visit to Michigan to see my family, Shelby, now two and a half, took my hand and asked, "Follow Shelby on yellow brick road?" I didn't know what she meant until her mother explained that Shelby was enchanted by *The Wizard of Oz*. They owned a video of the movie, and Shelby loved the story, was fascinated by the characters, and knew the words to several of the songs. She especially loved to sing "Somewhere Over the Rainbow."

I proceeded to follow Shelby around her house

singing, "We're off to see the Wizard, the wonderful Wizard of Oz." She'd prepared for our carefree, happy dancing walk on the yellow brick road by putting her jacket on and giving me two dolls to carry. She herself had two dolls in tow, along with a small dollhouse dog representing Toto. She showed me how to make the dolls dance by turning them from side to side. It was enchanting to see how her imagination orchestrated our journey down the yellow brick road. I was getting dizzy because we circled the sofa so many times, but she was the leader, and I followed. Finally, she took a new turn and we ended up in her playroom, filled with books and toys, a kitchen, and puzzles. She walked over to the far corner of the room, took off her jacket, and with eyes aglow and a huge smile, said, "We're here! We're in Emerald City. See Oz!" She was delightful!

The sparkle in her eyes was the magic of enchantment, which is what bliss is all about. I wish I could preserve it, bottle it. I believe we all can have it. We can claim it by the way we live our lives. We can claim it by practicing preventive health care. We can help our children retain it, teaching them by our example.

Ayurvedic philosophy takes a holistic approach to health care. It's the oldest holistic health plan that focuses on preventive medicine. As I stated earlier, according to Ayurveda, health is maintained by understanding and sustaining the delicate balance of the mind and body. For 5,000 years, practitioners of Ayurveda have recognized the link between the body and the mind and have known that we must be aware of both to maintain health. Unfortunately, this knowledge had been lost to the West.

In the 17th century, the philosopher and mathematician René Descartes introduced the concept of absolute separation of the mind from the body. This paradigm, called the *Cartesian method,* became a model for modern Western medicine. Medical research has adapted his concept of separating mind from body and applied it to the physician's role. The body is thought to be a well-made, complex machine, and if a person is sick, it's because one or more of the body parts isn't functioning properly. According to this mind-set, to restore health one merely has to fix the body part in question. The physician treats the symptom but never questions its cause. Known as *allopathic* medicine, this has become the dominant approach to health care in the West.

Today, Western medicine is just beginning to understand and recognize the interconnection of mind and body. Drs. Robert Ader and Nicholas Cohen, of the University of Rochester School of Medicine, conducted a series of experiments that prove there's an intimate relationship between the activity of the brain and the activity of the immune system. The study of this relationship is called *psychoneuroimmunology,* or PNI. PNI recognizes that every cell has intelligence and that the brain is not separate from the body. Every thought we have results in a chemical message in our brain. Called *neuropeptide,* this substance actually translates our thoughts into a material or physical state. Dr. Candace Pert, an eminent PNI researcher, says, "Your body is an outward manifestation of your mind." Mind and body are not separate and must be understood together. She calls this biochemical linkage bond *bodymind.*

Quantum mechanics is a branch of physics that goes beyond the physical and material orientation of the scientific method, and into a whole spectrum of the nonphysical. Quantum physicists have discovered a finite particle that's smaller than an atom. Named the *quark,* it appears to be the jumping-off point between the physical and the nonphysical. The quark is the spark that ignites thought. Thought determines our physical "realities," and the way we perceive "realities" molds our thoughts. The mind is more powerful than many of us have given it credit for. Without getting too technical or metaphysical, we can understand that there's more to health than a body being a functional, mechanical machine. The ingredients that help manifest good health encompass the human spirit, thoughts, and consciousness—in addition to the physical. Medical technology could serve us better if used in concert with the power of consciousness and positive thought.

Whereas allopathic Western medicine has made many technological advances, it has failed to include the entire dimension of the human spirit in its approach to healing. Ayurveda, however, takes a holistic approach to healing. It gives the responsibility for health back to the individual. The doctor's role can be likened to that of a symphony conductor. She helps the patient create health by directing him in blending and bringing into balance the various components of his life—diet, outlook, exercise, lifestyle.

In Ayurvedic medicine, the first step a physician will take is to give you a comprehensive evaluation of your mind/body type, so that recommendations can be made for diet, massage, exercise, and meditation. The specific recommendations will help the patient harmonize his physiological makeup with the demands of his lifestyle.

+++

About This Book

I believe that parenting begins at the moment of conception; therefore, the first chapter gives you guidelines and suggestions for maintaining a healthy, balanced lifestyle before and during pregnancy. It's only by being balanced yourself that the child in your womb can be so, too.

Chapter 2 explains individual constitutions or mind/body types—called *doshas* in Sanskrit—in detail. Every person has a combination of all three mind/body types, but in different ratios. Each dosha has positive attributes, along with weaknesses. The purpose of understanding your personal dosha ratio is to help you learn how to stay in a healthy balance. At the end of the chapter is a questionnaire that will help you discover your baby's mind/body type.

Various ways to center yourself and subsequently your child are discussed in Chapter 3. Centering is an important aspect of staying in balanced health. Stress can be an imbalance factor in your life, yet if you learn how to center yourself, you'll be on the path to preventing a negative reaction.

Chapter 4 introduces you to the healing aspects of touch. We all need touch in our lives, and medical research tells us that our little ones thrive both intellectually and physically when given loving touch. This chapter will teach you how to massage your baby with the best results.

Learning to use breath to cleanse the body and give it more energy is the focus of Chapter 5. And extending massage time to playful, simple yoga postures with your baby is a wonderful opportunity to introduce him or her to a lifelong exercise program.

In Chapter 6, I explain which foods are recommended and which aren't for each mind/body type. I talk about different ways to look at nutrition other than through foods, such as the consciousness of cooking.

Finally, Chapter 7 deals with a variety of ways to nurture yourself before, during, and after the birth of your baby, as well as throughout the postpartum period.

Although this book begins at the first stirrings of life and ends after the baby is born, I've applied the knowledge in each chapter to toddlers, and certainly you could apply it to older children. The questionnaire for adults to determine their dosha (also in Chapter 2) can be applied to a person of any age.

Raising happy and healthy children is every parent's wish. We all want to lead our children down a path of joy and well-being so that the vitality they have as youngsters remains with them their entire lives. Unfortunately, very few of us are sure how to do this. To my great delight, I discovered that Ayurveda has mapped out that route long ago. But taking the "road less traveled" in this part of the world makes it necessary for someone to make that road map accessible. This has been my goal: to provide a clear and practical set of guidelines for parents to use to make sure that their children have a blissful childhood and the tools necessary to carry that bliss throughout their lives.

+++   +++

+ + + + + + + +

CHAPTER 1

+ + + + + + + +

Courting Creation:
Keeping Mommy Balanced

*"What lies behind us and what lies before us
are tiny matters, compared to what lies within us."*

— Ralph Waldo Emerson

THE FIRST SECRET IS COURTING CREATION THROUGH A BALANCED MOTHER. Courting creation means bringing love into all aspects of your pregnancy. It's caring for the baby in your womb from the moment of conception. Under the best possible circumstances, you're the one who makes the choice to have a baby. In an ideal situation, you'll be practicing a balanced lifestyle, which includes eating nutritionally, getting enough rest, exercising moderately on a regular basis, and nurturing yourself. And you'll know how to relieve the stress in your life by practicing centering techniques.

In our hustle-and-bustle world of appointments, deadlines, and obligations, it's not always easy to take good care of ourselves. Sometimes, instead of taking the time to stop and enjoy our food, we eat while driving or stand at a counter and inhale our food. Often, we ignore the messages our bodies are trying to communicate to us. For example, we'll brush off our fatigue and try to combat it by having another cup of coffee. These are all unhealthy, stressful practices that need to be eliminated when we're pregnant.

The embryo feels stress if its mother is under stress. It feels disoriented when the mother is rushing through life. Now's the time to pay attention. A blissful baby comes from a contented and centered mother. Listen to the signals your body is sending you. Slow down. Eat more nutritious meals. Get more rest. Walk, don't run. Woo yourself through self-love.

In his book *Magical Child,* Joseph Chilton Pearce reminds us that the mother's womb offers three things to a newly forming life: a source of possibility, a source of energy to explore possibility, and a safe place within which that exploration can take place. In the womb, the infant is in a world of his own, his own universe in a sense. The perfection of the womb's design encourages physical and intellectual growth. It's one of the wonders of nature. As mothers, we're responsible for our child's universe. Our moods and reactions to things in our life are relayed chemically to the growing infant. It's easy to understand how vital the mother's states of mind, health, and emotion are. Everything the mother does and experiences is directly linked to the infant in utero. That's why it's so important to give up smoking and other unhealthful practices during pregnancy.

On a positive note, the best things we do are also transferred to the growing infant. Talking to your baby, telling her how much you love her, and playing beautiful music for her in utero all contribute to the baby's healthy development.

Mind/body connectiveness and consciousness are important not only for your own health, but for the future health of your baby. Make a promise to yourself today: Start listening to your body now! As a doctor friend of mine once told me, "The body of a pregnant woman asks for what it needs very loudly. The intuitive wisdom is there inside us, we just have to pay attention to it."

The concept that the body tells us what it needs really hit home with me recently as I thought back to my earlier years and the messages my body gave me that I refused to hear. When I was in college, between my schoolwork, dating, and the pressures of working 30-hour weeks, I was too busy (or so I thought) to sit down for a meal. It was my habit to eat on the run and ignore the signals my body was giving me. I remember getting "the shakes" on my way to class, and rushing toward a candy machine to buy a snack. My energy would peak for a few hours and then drop again as I was on my way to the shopping center where I held a sales job. Before going into the store, I'd pick up a caramel apple, and that would be my lunch. I can't believe it now, but I followed this pattern week after week after week.

One day, I felt my energy drop drastically as my boyfriend and I were on our way to a picnic. Quickly, I reached into our picnic basket and retrieved—then inhaled—a peanut butter sandwich. My boyfriend was angry at my rush to eat and called it impolite. My body was obviously out of balance, yet at the time I had no clue that it was really trying to tell me something.

Eventually I graduated from college and began working as an elementary school teacher. I was more excited about the cookies-and-milk break than the children in my kindergarten classroom. Like most young women, I had no idea that poor eating habits were the problem—or at least *part* of the problem. I continued eating erratically, and subsisted on a diet high in sugar to keep me going. I now know that those energy swings were my body's signals to get me back in balance.

I eventually married and got pregnant. My first pregnancy went very smoothly. My second one, two-and-a-half years later, had a different effect on my body. My nausea lasted at least five months. I'd be shopping in a mall with my first son, Marc, when I'd feel faint and have to sit down. I passed out on five different occasions. My sweet Marc stayed next to me, holding on to my leg, until I woke up. My doctor assured me it was normal. Although the sugar level in my urine was on the high side, it was within the normal range for pregnant women. Little by little, my symptoms increased. I was urinating more, and I had obsessive thirst. Leg cramps and charley horses occurred frequently. I felt lousy. In my sixth month, I looked like I could deliver any day; my stomach was huge, yet my limbs and face were quite thin.

Finally, on Christmas Eve, my doctor sent me to a clinic to take a five-hour glucose tolerance test. Three hours into the test, after having had blood taken three times, I regurgitated the remaining glucose. I was told I could leave but should return after the holidays.

By that time I was in my seventh month, and my doctor sent me to an endocrinologist who ordered another glucose tolerance test. This time I completed the test—but when the doctor saw the results, he immediately put me in the hospital and told me I had gestational diabetes. I didn't even know what diabetes was. I was in the hospital for a week, and I was really scared. They wouldn't release me until I learned how to give myself an insulin shot.

Finally, I overcame my fear and learned how to do this.

I was monitored twice a week for the next four weeks to see how the baby was developing. When a pregnant women has diabetes, the placenta (responsible for providing nourishment to the fetus) loses efficiency. The baby can starve to death if not watched carefully. If it were found that the placenta had lost efficiency, they would induce labor or take the baby by cesarean. Although I was scheduled to have a cesarean delivery, Ryan came on his own—five days before his scheduled delivery. He was born in my eighth month as a preemie, weighing nine and one-quarter pounds. (Diabetic mothers have very large babies.) Had Ryan gone to term, the doctor told me, he would have weighed around 12 pounds. (The term *preemie* refers to any newborn who has spent less than nine months in the womb.)

Today, Ryan is a strapping 25-year-old graduate of the University of California at Davis, with a degree in environmental studies. He's a very healthy young man, and both he and I were fortunate that my diabetes was caught early enough. But the question remains—could I have prevented the disease? I believe I could have. And if my body could have been brought back into balance, perhaps I wouldn't be taking insulin shots today. When the body is in balance, we can *prevent* as well as heal disease.

I now realize that had my daily schedule been more regulated, I could have avoided some of the health challenges I now have. In order to balance my body, I could have eaten meals calmly rather than on the run; chosen more nutritional foods; had more consistent sleep patterns, with fewer all-nighters; and set aside time daily for tuning my body. Many other things could have helped me balance my life, such as exercise, centering myself, and above all, knowing my mind/body type. All of these issues will be addressed in this book.

Mothers Need Nurturing, Too

In order to be balanced, we need to listen to our mind and body, pay attention to what we need, and respect ourselves enough to fulfill those needs. This is especially difficult for many women, as they're traditionally the nurturers and are conditioned to take care of others—not themselves. But we all need nurturing; it's one of our basic requirements as human beings.

This is particularly true for pregnant women, who are experiencing a myriad of physiological changes and are assaulted by conflicting messages from themselves and the culture. As a new life grows inside of them, they may feel beautiful, alive, and sexy, but many people in our society see motherhood and sexuality as disparate images. They're uncomfortable thinking of a mother as a sexual being. A pregnant woman may internalize this and may begin to hate her body because of the changes it's going through. She may feel fat and unattractive. As the pregnant woman goes through one of the most miraculous and rewarding experiences her body is capable of—giving form to and sustaining life—society may view her as fragile and less capable of functioning physically and emotionally.

To combat these negative perceptions, a pregnant woman needs to remain centered and feel good about herself; she needs to be nurtured by others, and most important, by *herself*.

The story I'm going to share with you comes from a woman who didn't have the nurturing she needed. This is a very touching story from a Desert Storm Navy nurse, Dani Newman, regarding her own pregnancy. A variety of factors caused an emotional imbalance in Dani, which led to an uncentered pregnancy and subsequently a detached feeling toward her baby.

As a Naval nurse, I'd worked in labor and delivery, and I had witnessed a hundred births. One Christmas when I was overseas in Japan, I had tears in my eyes taking a picture of the first baby boy born on Christmas Day that year. I'm still very attached to that moment. Another woman named her ninth son after me, so I had a history of being involved in the birthing process.

When my first pregnancy occurred, I was living geographically apart from my husband because of the job I had to do. I was very attached to this first pregnancy. Due to the emotional stress of living apart from my husband, I miscarried at 12 weeks. When I lost that baby, it was an emotional time for me. . . . About six weeks after the miscarriage, I got pregnant again with my daughter. I had a great deal of bleeding with the second pregnancy and kept thinking I was going to lose this baby, too. It was a traumatic time for me. Because I was 35 and considered an older woman, I had to have several medical tests. I had an amniocentesis as well as other genetic testing because my husband had a sister with Down syndrome. His family also had a history of Tay-Sachs. I kept bleeding. Emotionally I was stressed out. I'd moved that week from Orange County, California, to San Diego. On top of it, that was the week I got recalled to Desert Storm.

Dani was under an enormous amount of stress, and she feared another miscarriage. Her stoic attitude covered up her grief; she just put on a stiff upper lip and went on her way in front of her comrades.

> *Because I was afraid of another miscarriage, I never really attached myself to the pregnancy. I was very distanced from it. In a strange way, being in the military was the best part of the pregnancy. The women I worked with were so caring.*
>
> *By the third month of my pregnancy, I was out of the service. The war was over. I was discharged. At that point, I was almost in total denial of myself and my pregnancy. I was going back to a job that had been held open for me for six months. I went back to a senior management job in health care. It wasn't said in words, but I felt as if they were saying, "How could you do this to us? We saved this job for you for six months and now you come back pregnant." I felt a lot of stress, and I told myself over and over, "This baby is not going to affect my job."*
>
> *I felt very insecure. I didn't have a nurturing environment. My family all lived far from me. I had no immediate friends that I could share the pregnancy with. Even my husband wasn't there for me in a supportive manner. I felt alone. My body began to swell and swell. In the past I was a size four, and now I was over 200 pounds. I had to stuff my feet into the only pair of shoes that still fit me. I was rejecting how I looked. My husband was rejecting me as well. So in turn, the baby was rejected, especially after I found out it was a girl. My husband and I had both wanted a boy. . . . It was a very negative experience. I don't think I ever felt lonelier.*

Dani was depressed and remained detached from her newborn baby. It took a full year for her to bond with her daughter. This realization hit her like a ton of bricks when she took her daughter to a Disney movie.

The movie was about this little girl lost in a forest. There was a search party, and the mother and father were also looking for the little girl. The mother was frantic. Well, the dog and cat found the little girl and started barking. The father and mother, yelling out the little girl's name, ran over to where the dog had the child. I started sobbing and reached over to my little girl and held her so tight. I realized then how attached I was to my daughter. It had taken me a full year to bond with her emotionally.

Dani's story is a perfect example of being out of touch with your mind/body connection. Pregnancy is a time when we must make a special effort to ensure that this doesn't happen. How easy it is to let outside expectations color our world. Dani's dismal outlook could have changed if only she'd had a support system, time to nurture herself, and a husband who was sensitive to what she was going through.

Having a plan for self-nurturing is a good way to prepare for pregnancy. When you think of ways to nurture yourself during pregnancy, you are in turn planning the ways your baby will also be nurtured. Your emotional needs, feelings, and concerns are felt by the baby. So, seek out and set up a support system to handle your questions, your fears, and your excitement. Talk to your husband or partner so that you can share your journey. Don't leave your partner out by keeping problems hidden. Make a conscious effort to allow this time to be special, no matter how stressful your life may seem.

IN CONTRAST TO DANI'S STORY, Debbie Graefer's story demonstrates a more centered way of handling stress during pregnancy. Debbie's practice of Kriya Yoga meditation (which consists of very deep breathing exercises) was and continues to be the foundation for her stability. This method, as well as other meditative techniques, help to unite the mind, body, and spirit.

Debbie, a doctor of Oriental medicine and an acupuncturist, moved from the Northeast to California with her daughter and husband. They left the comforts of their own home, their close family, and their roots. However, Debbie and her husband had a very nurturing relationship, which kept her centered throughout the many difficulties she encountered.

I was geared toward having my own house, but when we got out here, we were renting and it bothered me. My husband, Clause, was ill with cancer at the time, and we were strapped financially. Even so, every once in a while we'd go to an open house on a Sunday. I'd see it and then would pray afterwards that we'd have a house of our own soon. We'd come back to our rented house, and I'd say, "You know what? This is really perfect, and I'm grateful for what I have, but when I'm pregnant, I want a house." I said that every time that we went looking.

We were both very optimistic back then, and we wanted another child. One night in front of the fireplace, we made love. The next morning we got a phone call from Germany; my husband's father, Albrecht, had passed away. We made immediate arrangements to leave. Later we went through all the questions about where we were at the time of his death. Oddly enough, we were in front of the fireplace making love. So we said, "Wouldn't it be funny if we conceived at that time, too?"

We went to Germany, and three weeks later I was getting all these weird cravings. On the way back, we stopped in Toronto to see my family, and I had a pregnancy test. Yes, I was pregnant. The interesting thing was that my father-in-law left us $50,000. It was enough for a down payment on a house. What did I say the moment I was conceiving? "When I get pregnant, I want a house." You know, it happened within an hour, almost to the minute. Things like that always happen in my life. It's so wonderful to see how accurate it can be. It's the kind of thing that makes life worthwhile. I got my house to be pregnant in.

Then the worst thing happened: My husband died from the cancer. People had a hard time seeing me pregnant and losing my husband. I can't tell you what a blessing it was just to have this new life inside me. There was certainly difficulty afterward. I didn't know if I could raise the baby alone without the love and attention of its father. Having a baby, though, gives you reason to go on. You have this child in your arms, you're nursing it all these hours, so you have affection, touching, and so on.

This is a good example of a woman in one of the worst situations, grieving and alone, yet her connection to her baby and herself was so strong that she made it through the challenge. Symbolically, Debbie's home was what nurtured her, and it gave her a sense of stability for the family. Working in her garden was another way she nurtured herself, as she watched her new future take root.

Nurture Your Baby by Nurturing Yourself

Nurturing yourself during pregnancy isn't a luxury, it's a necessity. Our society makes us feel guilty if we take time out for ourselves. Instead of being pressured by "shoulds," think of how enjoyable it will be to create an enriching pregnancy. Focus time and attention on yourself at this special time. If you have other children, you need to set aside special time for them, too—but don't neglect *your* needs.

Charaka, an ancient Ayurvedic physician, said that "a baby is made up of four components: one part mother, one part father, one part of the mother's intake during pregnancy, and one part from a generalized aspect of nature or consciousness."[1] Intake during pregnancy is the one aspect over which we have direct control. It consists of food, drink, the air we breathe, perceptions, thoughts, and feelings.

The most vital nourishment a baby can have is the mother's happiness. According to Ayurveda, emotions are as important as your physiology during pregnancy. The books you read, as well as the movies you watch, impact the life inside you. The people you associate with have a direct effect on your emotions—therefore, it's best to stay away from negative people. Support groups are especially significant at this time. Society today is very mobile, so the assistance and comfort that was traditionally provided by extended families has been entrusted to peers. Find a support group that fits your needs.

Emotional changes during pregnancy are normal

because your hormones are changing. Mood swings and conflicting feelings, from being thrilled one minute to being terrified the next, are all very natural. Fears of labor and how you'll cope with pain can be dealt with by talking to other pregnant women and mothers who have also experienced those same fears. Again, support groups are very reassuring, because they help you realize that your fears are not unique, they're universal.

If you're married or have a partner in your life, your mate can be an incredible asset. Giving you extra attention and affection during this time is an important contribution to the development of your child. It helps to keep you happy. Staying home as much as possible in the evening helps you get the rest you need during your pregnancy. Rest is vital at this special time.

Exercise is also important to your well-being. Thirty minutes of daily walking is ideal for the pregnant woman. Running should be avoided, as should weight lifting or straining. Swimming is a fine exercise for total aerobic fitness, as it eliminates the pressures of gravity that may cause stress in your joints.

Taking time out to meditate when pregnant is a great advantage. Initially, you may say you don't have the time, or you can't be quiet for that long, but once you experience the benefits of meditation, you'll cherish the time you've set aside. Meditation is a way of centering yourself that increases productivity and provides a deep rest that boosts your energy level. (Chapter 3 will discuss meditation in detail, explaining its advantages and benefits.) The importance and value of meditation will continue long after you've delivered your baby. It will set a rhythm to your life from which you'll reap many rewards.

Ayurveda recommends a daily practice of self-massage

with oil during pregnancy. The skin is the largest organ in the body, and it stimulates healing endorphins when touched. Massage aids in relaxing the muscles, lubricating the tissues, and loosening the joints, as well as stimulating flexibility. The practice of daily oil massage is called *abhyanga*. I have personally found that it wakes me up and is an ideal pre-shower ritual. It also puts me in touch with my body, making me aware of areas I need to concentrate on when exercising.

Another thing you can do is to have your mate, or even a friend, give you a massage. Touch is very intimate, so at a time when sensitivities are increased and emotions are running the gamut, interpersonal communication through touch will help. Your mate or friend will be helping you ease your discomfort, and your bond will deepen.

Sesame oil is most commonly used for massage. Almond, olive, or coconut oil may take its place. It's recommended that you heat the oil on low heat until it's just warm. Make sure that each time you apply the oil, it's still heated. Apply a small amount of oil to the head, face, and neck area first. Continue with the entire body massage, in circular motion, around joints, like elbows and knees, and finish with the feet.

Jennifer Louden, in *The Pregnant Woman's Comfort Book,* emphasizes being true to yourself, playful, and centered. In one of her exercises, she says, "Complete this sentence as many times as you can, as quickly as you can: *To feel nurtured and taken care of during my pregnancy, I need . . .*"[2] She continues by suggesting that you perform an exercise listing your needs, how you can meet your needs, and who can help you meet those needs. You can use the following example to make your own list, adjusted to fit your situation.

Need	How Can I Meet This Need?	Who Can Help Me?
Daily Walks	Commit to share walk time	Partner, husband, friend
Meditation	Meditation tapes, music, class	Instructor, pregnant friend
Nutrition	Ready-packaged, clean produce	Health-food store
	Read nutrition books	Librarian

After writing a list with 20 or more needs, think about and list ways to fulfill each need.

Another wonderful resource book is *The Artist's Way*, by Julia Cameron, which helps people break through their creative blocks to discover and recover their creative selves. The author suggests that you make a list of your 20 favorite things to do, and then date the last time you did each of them. I personally got a great deal out of that exercise. I was amazed by how many things I love to do but haven't done for years. Make a date with yourself once a week: Visit that gallery, go to the zoo with or without your mate, or get a massage. You deserve to be good to yourself, so give yourself permission. The baby you're creating will benefit, because every time you feel happy, endorphins will be manufactured and excreted within your body. The baby will receive these endorphins, too. This is a great way to make your baby happy and content.

Many of your fears and doubts about being a good parent can be resolved by thinking ahead and deciding what gifts you want your child to receive from you. Jennifer Louden calls it a "Life Pledge." Make a list of life promises you wish to give. Discuss them with your mate, friends, or family. The process alone will give you a feeling of stability. You'll begin to feel a new confidence about parenting. Visualize the happy, playful things you want to share with your baby, and again you'll feel more confidence and competence in parenting.

We're gifted with a child, to be his or her loving teacher, to prepare that child for life. Let us take pride in preparing that Life Pledge, and use it as a model to follow. Make pledges to your new baby at a naming ceremony, religious ceremony (christening), or personal family ceremony you create yourself. In doing so, your Life Pledge becomes anchored.

Turn past disappointment into positive affirmations. Here's an example from my life: My father always made promises to take me to the circus or to a parade, but when the time came, he either forgot or wasn't up to going. My pledge was to make keeping promises a priority. Imagination is the key, so let your imagination flourish with fantasy. Take out all those boxed-up wishes you had when you were a child and make them happen for you and your new baby in your mind's eye. Every thought becomes a seed in gestation and can come true someday.

Pregnancy is a rich time for insights. Writing in a journal is the best way to clarify and map out our feelings, whether they be about our relationship to our grandmothers or mothers, or just about our passages in pregnancy. A journal can be as simple a thing as a ringed school notebook with lined paper, or as fancy as a leather (or lace) book designed for the purpose. Keep a record of your journey. Maternity is a time for reflecting on "being pregnant."

Looking back to my pregnancies 20-some years ago, I wish I'd had the insight to write down my thoughts and feelings. I kept everything to myself. I didn't even share my feelings with my husband. It was a different time. The women I knew weren't in support groups, and their mates were too busy building businesses or practices to sit down and listen. During my second pregnancy, when I became diabetic, I was very frightened and had no one to turn to or to share my fears with. If I'd kept a journal, I would have had a means of expressing my feelings. So, don't bottle up your feelings, because they affect your baby. Writing down thoughts, feelings, and insights can provide a real catharsis.

Living in the Moment

One of the most important ways to nurture yourself is to pay attention to yourself, and one of the best ways to do that is by living in the moment rather than projecting into the future or reliving your past through memories. Neither is as proactive and as healthy as keeping your attention on the present moment. That's why it's called the *present—* because it's such a gift. Almost every spiritual teaching, including Christianity, Islam, Judaism, and the Vedic teaching of India, espouses the philosophy that existing in the *present moment* is the best way to live and to appreciate life.

Many years ago, I read a book called *Be Here Now* by the Lama Foundation's editor, Ram Dass; it awakened me to the benefits of living in the present. Over the years, this teaching has been confirmed over and over in my life. Are there ways to train ourselves to pay attention and to live fully in the present moment? Indeed there are. Taking the time to sit and make something with your hands focuses that time on the present. Beading a necklace or taking a picture can bring your attention to the present moment. Another suggestion is delicious, nutritious, and productive all in one—it's to practice the ritual of cooking from a color wheel. The goal is to bring together many different colors and textures into a single meal—using vegetables, fruits, grains, and proteins. Revel in the experience, and let your senses keep you grounded in the present.

If you can be in the present moment with your children, then you'll experience the best that motherhood has to offer. If you become so caught up in the "shoulds" of motherhood, you won't notice the little miracles that come along many times a day. The joy of motherhood comes with being flexible in the moment. Laugh at the snarls, and go on to the next adventure in your day. All any of us can do is our best.

Life is funny, and sometimes the best-made plans go astray. Sometimes circumstance can interfere with our well-being and we don't have a clue how to get back on track. This book is going to assist you by giving you knowledge about balancing your body and keeping it in balance.

It's taken me 24 years to gain enough knowledge to figure out how to stay balanced—emotionally, physically, and spiritually. Yoga, meditation, and touch have all provided me with wonderful tools for creating balance in my life. But learning Ayurveda has had the *most* profound effect on me because it weaves everything together under one health system. Through Ayurveda, I've gained an understanding of mind/body types, how to pay constructive attention to my body's symptoms, and how to take practical and preventive actions for my health. The effects of Ayurveda in my life have been far-reaching.

Summary

- + Ayurveda is an ancient Indian preventive-health system.

- + It's the oldest holistic health system that integrates mind and body.

- + It's important to listen kindly to what our bodies tell us.

- + When the body is emotionally, physically, and spiritually in balance, there's no room for disease.

- + In utero, the growing infant internalizes all the mother's emotions—good, bad, and indifferent.

- + Nurturing yourself during pregnancy isn't a luxury but a necessity.

- + A mother's happiness during pregnancy is a baby's most vital nourishment.

- + Meditation during pregnancy gives you more energy and increases productivity.

- + Keep a journal to record your insights, your feelings, and your dreams while pregnant.

+++ +++

✦ ✦ ✦ ✦ ✦ ✦ ✦ ✦

CHAPTER 2

✦ ✦ ✦ ✦ ✦ ✦ ✦ ✦

Discovering Your Baby's Mind/ Body Type: Diagnosing and Working with Doshas

"The blueprint for perfect health is inside you."

— Deepak Chopra

THE SECOND SECRET IS FINDING OUT YOUR BABY'S MIND/BODY TYPE. According to Charaka, an ancient Ayurvedic physician, "health results from the natural, balanced state of the dosha. Therefore, the wise try to keep them in a balanced state."[1] The immune system of healthy, balanced people helps them resist disease more effectively than those who are out of balance. Ayurveda is complementary to Western medicine because it provides a preventive approach to health—the focus is on keeping us in balance. When our body, mind, and spirit are in balance, we're healthy and happy, settled in our selves, and able to nurture our baby effortlessly. A simple ancient Ayurvedic truth is, "If a parent is happy, then the child will be happy."

During pregnancy, it's especially important to stay healthy. Knowing your dosha (mind/body type) and following the recommendations for your constitution will keep you balanced—and, therefore, in good health. It's important to understand the doshas and to learn about the characteristics of each so that we can recognize when we're out of balance.

Everything in the universe can be described in terms of the three doshas—called *Vata*, *Pitta*, and *Kapha*. Between them, these three principles encompass every quality and characteristic—and are evident in every type of being that exists. From seasons to appetites, from foods to body types and personalities, knowledge of the three doshas can help our understanding of the world.

We all have some of each dosha in us. One dosha is usually more dominant than the others, although sometimes two doshas dominate more or less equally. An individual is rarely influenced by all three in equal measure. For our purposes, it will be helpful to refer to people who are Vata-dominant, for example, as simply *Vatas*.

To recognize an imbalance in yourself, it's important that you be familiar with the characteristics of all three of the doshas, and discover which is your own primary dosha. By doing so, you'll be alerted to tendencies in many areas—including specific illnesses you're prone to. This knowledge, of course, will help you to take appropriate preventive care, for you'll be able to recognize the symptoms of an imbalance, and thus identify its source and remedy it. So, in order to be "brought into balance," you must identify which dosha needs adjustment (usually it will be the primary one, but not always).

The following charts list the main characteristics of the three doshas, as well as symptoms they tend to exhibit when imbalanced, and the correct measures to help identify them.

VATA CHARACTERISTICS

MIND
enthusiastic personality
learns quickly
restless/active mind

BODY
cold hands and feet
dry skin
thin physique

VATA IMBALANCE

SYMPTOMS
worry/anxiety
constipation
insomnia

CORRECTIONS
quiet
regular routines
warmth (warm foods)

A Vata imbalance can most easily be corrected by a regular routine including quiet time (meditation or silence). The spontaneous, excitable energy of Vata needs scheduling.

PITTA CHARACTERISTICS

MIND
articulate
sharp intellect
precise, orderly

BODY
perspires easily
red hair, early baldness
freckled skin

PITTA IMBALANCE

SYMPTOMS
rashes, blemishes, ulcers
impatience
hot flashes (red in face)

CORRECTIONS
moderation
decrease in stimulants
cool foods, staying cool

A Pitta imbalance can most easily be corrected by moderation. Pittas gravitate toward extremes, and their energy tends to be intense; therefore, setting reasonable limits is the best way to get it back into balance.

KAPHA CHARACTERISTICS

<u>MIND</u>
calm, easygoing
slow to learn
great memory

<u>BODY</u>
gains weight easily
good stamina, sturdy
sleeps deeply

KAPHA IMBALANCE

<u>SYMPTOMS</u>
sinus congestion,
  allergies
diabetes
high cholesterol

<u>CORRECTIONS</u>
stimulation
regular exercise
weight control

A Kapha imbalance can best be corrected by stimulation. Kaphas tend to get lethargic, and their energy is slow and deliberate. Therefore, exercise and spicy foods—or an injection of excitement—will spark their energy and help balance them.

DENISE, A VATA-DOMINANT FRIEND OF MINE who recently went through a divorce, moved twice in one year with her two young daughters and was in the middle of writing a book when she became totally imbalanced. She couldn't sleep, and her emotions were very raw. When she started to have minor car accidents due to a lack of concentration, I suggested meditation and exercise. She's now back in balance, using Aikido (a Japanese martial art) and meditation as her routine stabilizers.

A Pitta-dominant friend of mine named Mitch tends to go to extremes when working or playing. Recently hooked up to the Internet, he often stays online until three or four in the morning. When a tree was blown over in the yard, he spent the next day sawing up tree limbs until his face was as red as a beet. And to top it off, his work schedule had him up late at night and early in the morning. He was very imbalanced, which caused a skin rash. I suggested a cold shower and a dish of ice cream (Pittas can't resist ice cream). Immediately after taking these measures, he calmed down, his complexion began to stabilize, and he saw the error of his extremist ways. I also suggested that he slow down and do things in moderation. Later, he got some rest and began to set limits on his time on the Internet. Again, I could visibly witness the positive effects of these steps toward balance. But Mitch will always have to challenge himself to set limits because of his Pitta dominance.

My son Ryan has a Kapha-dominant body type. He has a stocky, muscular build and a great deal of stamina. The only time I remember him feeling imbalanced was when he was in college. He was under a great deal of academic stress and had no time to exercise, which made him sluggish. I told him to eat spicy foods and try to fit in some kind of exercise. After graduation, he got back on a rigorous workout program and feels better than ever. His energy level is much higher than it was when he was unable to exercise.

Although the three doshas are clearly distinct types, no one is exclusively one or another. Usually we have a dominant dosha in combination with another dosha (or doshas)—for example, Vata-Pitta (or Pitta-Vata); Pitta-Kapha (or Kapha-Pitta); Vata-Kapha (or Kapha-Vata); or the most unusual, a combination of the three, Vata-Pitta-Kapha.

Barbara Manley Wheeler, R.N., M.S., an Ayurveda

practitioner for many years, shared some valuable comments on how doshas may change balance during pregnancy.

Studying the doshas can help us stay healthy. In the first trimester of pregnancy, especially when your hormones are changing and a new life is growing inside you, it's normal to get an imbalance that would affect the Vata first of all. (The dosha that's most strongly affected is the Vata because it's the strongest one.) Having some nausea and being very tired is definitely a Vata imbalance. In the middle trimester, everything seems to balance out. In my own pregnancies—and I've had five—those middle three months were the best of my entire life. Women look so beautiful in this middle phase of pregnancy.

However, in my fourth pregnancy, I was listening to my body very closely, and it felt strange. I had more nausea and heartburn than I'd had in my other pregnancies. I wasn't sleeping and had constipation. These changes had a big effect on me, and by just listening to my body, I knew something was different: My Vata was extremely out of balance.

Although the doctors didn't know it until the delivery, I was pregnant with twins. I knew that I certainly had more imbalances than I'd had in my other pregnancies, but I didn't know why. In retrospect, it was because I had two babies and two placentas. The babies weighed five pounds, eleven ounces; and five pounds, thirteen ounces.

It's important to study all three doshas to get an understanding of your body, and to then follow steps to bring your dosha back in balance. Of course, this won't happen overnight—it's a process. Listening and understanding gives you a closer look at your body so you can ask, "What's my body trying to say to me? What's going on with me?" When you meditate, you'll also get intuitive answers that will help you balance your doshas.

Your body will tell you what it needs. Once you start listening to it, you'll give it what it wants in moderation—like a couple of potato chips, but not the whole bag. Then you'll create balance.

If both parents are in a balanced state before pregnancy, then there's additional assurance that the baby will be balanced. In Ayurveda, it's suggested that the prospective father—as well as the mother—follow a certain lifestyle, including dietary and cleansing procedures for balancing his doshas before conception.

In the following pages, you'll find a questionnaire to help you determine what your dosha makeup is. Remember that even though you can understand yourself better by knowing your primary dosha, it's best to learn about all three doshas so that you can adjust your imbalances. People have a tendency to think of their primary dosha as if it were their sun sign, but being a Pitta isn't like being a Libra or a Scorpio. With the doshas, it's important to understand all three types in order to have the ability to recognize when they're out of balance and to then correct those imbalances. Such a comprehensive understanding of the doshas provides an invaluable preventive health tool.

✦✦✦

Place check off the choices that best describe you.

VATA	PITTA	KAPHA
– Thin and can be unusually tall or short	– Medium, well-proportioned frame	– Tend to be ample in build
– Thin as a child	– Medium build as child	– Plump or a little chunky in childhood
– Light bones, prominent joints	– Medium bone structure	– Heavy bone structure
– Have a hard time gaining weight	– Can gain or lose weight easily, if you put your mind to it	– Gain weight easily, have a hard time losing it
– Small, active, dark eyes	– Penetrating light green, gray, blue, or amber eyes	– Large, attractive eyes with thick eyelashes
– Dry skin, chaps easily	– Oily skin and hair	– Tan slowly but usually evenly, skin stays cool longer than most
– Dark, dry, thick hair	– Fair skin, sunburn easily	– Thick, wavy hair, a little oily, dark or light
– Prefer warm climate, sunshine, moisture	– Fine, light, oily hair; blond, red, or early gray or early balding	– Any climate is fine as long as it's not too humid
– Variable appetite, can get very hungry, but may find "eyes bigger than stomach"	– Prefer cool, well-ventilated places	– Like to eat, fine appetite, but can skip meals without physical problems if necessary (not that they like to)
– Bowel movements can be irregular, hard, dry, or constipated	– Irritable if you miss a meal or can't eat when you are hungry; good appetite	– Regular daily bowel movements; steady, thick, heavy
– Digestion sometimes good and sometimes not	– Easy and regular bowel movements; if anything, soft, oily, loose stools at least once or twice a day	– Digestion fine, sometimes a little slow
– Dislike routine	– Usually good digestion	– Work well with routine
– Creative thinker	– Enjoy planning and like routine, especially if you create it	– Good at keeping an organization or project running smoothly
– Feel more mentally relaxed when exercising	– Good initiator and leader	
– Change your mind easily	– Exercise helps keep emotions from going out of control	

- Tend toward fear or anxiety under stress
- Often dream, but rarely remember your dreams
- Changeable moods and ideas
- Like to snack, nibble
- If ill, nervous disorders or sharp pain most likely
- Light sleeper
- Think that money is there to be spent
- Sexual interest variable, fantasy life active
- Brittle nails
- Cold hands and feet, little perspiration
- Thin, fast, variable pulse
- Variable thirst

- Have opinions and like to share them
- Tend toward anger, frustration, irritability under stress
- Relatively easy to remember dreams, often dream in color
- Forceful about expressing ideas and feelings
- Enjoy high-protein foods like chicken, fish, eggs, and beans
- If ill, fevers, rashes, inflammation more likely
- Usually sleep well
- Think money is best spent on special items or on purchases that will advance you
- Ready sexual energy and drive
- Nails flexible but pretty strong
- Good circulation, perspire frequently, warm hands
- Strong, full pulse
- Usually thirsty

- Exercise keeps your weight down in a way diet won't
- Change your mind slowly
- Tend to avoid difficult situations
- Generally only remember dreams if they're especially intense or significant
- Steady, reliable, slow to change
- Love fatty and starchy foods
- If ill, excess fluid retention or mucus more likely
- Sound, heavy sleeper
- Money is easy to save
- Steady sexual interest and drive
- Strong, thick nails
- Moderate perspiration, cool hands
- Steady, slow, rhythmic pulse
- Rarely thirsty

Add up all your check marks. The mind/body type (constitution) with the most check marks indicates your primary dosha. If you've marked two constitutions nearly as often, you may be a *dual dosha*. Rarely, all three will be relatively equal, in which case a *tri-dosha*, Vata-Pitta-Kapha-type results.[2] Reprinted with permission, *The Ayurvedic Cookbook*, Amadea Morningstar and Urmila Desai, Lotus Press, P.O. Box 325, Twin Lakes, MI 53181. © 1990, All rights reserved.

+ + +

"All you need to receive guidance is to ask for it,
and then listen."

— Sanaya Roman

Why is this information so important? Well, it can help us maintain our body's balance. And balance, after all is said and done, is the key to health. Particular combinations of energies are present when we're born; what we do with those energies after birth is up to us. Knowing how those energies work can provide a blueprint for our health and a lifetime of vitality and well-being; on the other hand, ignoring them can be a direct route to low energy and deteriorating health.

Dr. Atsuko Rees, from the Maharishi Ayur-Veda Center in Pacific Palisades, California, told me in an interview, "One of our recommendations is that mothers and babies stay home for the first 40 days." This may sound strange or impractical given our modern lifestyle habits, but it's an important part of the mother's recovery and will give her more strength to deal with the demands of motherhood in the future. Some women never give themselves enough time to rebuild their bodies and replenish their strength.

Babies also need time to adjust to their new environment. For nine months, they've thrived in an insulated, protected womb. Birth can be a traumatic event, and once they arrive, everything is different. For one thing, nutrition isn't automatic anymore. And there are many other adjustments for the baby to make as well. So quiet time at home is highly beneficial because it allows both baby and mother to adjust to and integrate all of the new experiences that begin at birth. Those first 40 days are also the ideal time to begin close observation of your baby as you get to know each other.

Discovering Your Baby's Dosha

Ten days after a baby's birth is the earliest time a baby's mind/body type can be determined. After ten days, the doshas have had time to rebalance from birth. When your baby is more than ten days old, you can look for signs that will help determine his or her mind/body type. However, this is rarely done at this time. Dr. Rees says, "It is said that babies predominately have a Kapha dosha, and it isn't until later in the first year, when they're eating table food and walking, that their personal predominances come out." The baby's dosha is best determined by observing different patterns—eating, sleeping, sensitivity to noise, interaction with others—as well as personality characteristics.

There are two ways to get a more definitive interpretation of your baby's mind/body type: One is to take your baby to a medical practitioner trained in Ayurveda. But if you live in a part of the country where it's difficult to find an Ayurvedic practitioner, you can use the questionnaire that appears later in this chapter. By discussing mind/body types with Ayurveda doctors, and through my own personal observation and knowledge of babies, I put together this comprehensive questionnaire to help you determine your baby's dosha. It will help you focus your attention and observations. You'll find that the questionnaire is even more beneficial and accurate when your baby is six months old or older.

If you *do* have access to an Ayurvedic practitioner, here's what you can expect. The practitioner will use pulse diagnosis to determine the general state of health of the baby. Pulse is intimately related to mind/body type. The fastest pulse is Vata, and it also has an irregular beat. Ayurveda likens the Vata type of pulse to a snake. The forceful throbbing pulse of Pitta has a medium rate—it's slower than Vata, but quicker than Kapha. Its rhythm is likened to a frog. The Kapha pulse is typically slow, smooth, and sliding—and likened to a swan.

In Ayurvedic pulse diagnosis, a female's pulse is taken on the left arm and a male's pulse is taken on the right arm. Three fingers are used, each finger representing a different mind/body pulse. All three pulses are present in everyone, and the technique of Ayurveda pulse recognizes each of them and identifies the most prominent signal. This technique is different from traditional Western pulse-taking because it's more specific, with each finger pressing lightly on the radial artery in different locations. A skilled Ayurvedic physician or pulse reader can assess your baby's pulse. If anything is out of balance, the practitioner can address what needs to be done to get the baby back into alignment.

I had the opportunity to spend a week with my grandbaby, Shelby, when she was eight months old. She'd changed a great deal since my previous visit. She was crawling, standing, and on the verge of walking. Although her teeth hadn't come in yet, she was eating small, cut-up portions of a vast assortment of table foods. Shelby's personality had developed, along with definite preferences for specific foods and activities.

It was during this visit that I got a true sense of which dosha is predominant in her nature. She loved ice cream and preferred cool liquids to lukewarm ones. Those few inclinations gave me a hint that she was developing Pitta characteristics. Yet her thick, dark hair; easygoing disposition; and deep and sound sleep patterns indicated a strong Kapha constitution. Her even temper and cuddly nature further implied a Kapha predominance. At that point, it seemed as if Shelby was a Kapha-Pitta.

On my next visit to Michigan, Shelby was ten months old. This time I had the opportunity to accompany Alisa, my daughter-in-law, and Shelby to their first appointment with an Ayurvedic physician. After filling out the usual forms, we were ushered into a room where we were instructed to listen to an audiotape on the practices and philosophy of Ayurveda. The doctor invited us into her office when we finished listening to the tape. She took Shelby's small wrist and took deliberate care to study her pulse. Dr. Ready assured us that Shelby was balanced and in optimum health. She, too, saw the Kapha dominance, but wasn't fully convinced of another dosha at this time.

Dr. Ready made extensive dietary recommendations (which I describe further in Chapter 6). One of these was to start boiling organic milk with a small amount of ginger when Shelby turned one year old. This was to help the milk digest properly and to eliminate gas. My daughter-in-law saw the value of this preventive approach to health, and also appreciated the suggestion of using aromatherapy oil for Shelby at her bedtime to calm and relax the baby. Another valuable recommendation was to do baby massage. My daughter-in-law and I smiled at each other because we were ahead of the game—Alisa had been giving massages to Shelby for several months.

Whether you'll be working with an Ayurvedic physician or diagnosing your baby's doshas on your own, an easy rule of thumb when watching for imbalances in your child is to notice when she is acting different and looking uncomfortable. A rash would indicate an obvious Pitta imbalance, but other imbalances may be more subtle. Watch for any signs of change. Being familiar with the characteristics of each dosha, you'll be able to determine what's out of balance and what's needed to remedy the imbalance. Awareness of your child's needs, and meeting those needs, assures balance and a happy and healthy life for your baby.

+++

"Your body is the ground metaphor of your life, the expression of your existence."

— Gabrielle Roth

In this questionnaire, you'll evaluate how well each characteristic describes your baby. Fill out all three sections; you can then determine separate Vata, Pitta, and Kapha scores. Using an agreement scale from 0 to 6, simply circle the number that best fits your response to each item; 0 means "no agreement" and 6 means "most highly agreed."

+++

YOUR BABY'S MIND/BODY TYPE

VATA	
My baby gets irritable when chilled.	0 1 2 3 4 5 6
My baby is most happy when the weather is warm.	0 1 2 3 4 5 6
My baby gets overstimulated easily.	0 1 2 3 4 5 6
My baby's hands and feet tend to get cold easily.	0 1 2 3 4 5 6
My baby gets gas easily.	0 1 2 3 4 5 6
My baby has difficulty falling asleep or having a sound sleep.	0 1 2 3 4 5 6
My baby's energy seems to come in bursts.	0 1 2 3 4 5 6
My baby prefers warm or room-temperature liquids.	0 1 2 3 4 5 6
My baby responds to light and bright colors.	0 1 2 3 4 5 6
My baby's bowel movements are irregular, either loose or constipated.	0 1 2 3 4 5 6
My baby is a light sleeper.	0 1 2 3 4 5 6
My baby is thinner than most babies.	0 1 2 3 4 5 6

My baby likes to nibble or snack.	0 1 2 3 4 5 6
My baby has dry skin.	0 1 2 3 4 5 6
My baby is very physically active.	0 1 2 3 4 5 6
My baby's hair tends to be curly and wiry.	0 1 2 3 4 5 6
My baby sleeps less than most other babies.	0 1 2 3 4 5 6
My baby has an irregular appetite.	0 1 2 3 4 5 6
My baby likes sour tastes.	0 1 2 3 4 5 6
My baby performs activities quickly.	0 1 2 3 4 5 6

Add up your baby's Vata points: _____

PITTA	
My baby prefers cold liquids, not warm.	0 1 2 3 4 5 6
My baby tends toward loose and frequent bowel movements.	0 1 2 3 4 5 6
My baby is persistent and never gives up trying to do something.	0 1 2 3 4 5 6
My baby is hungry frequently and eats frequently.	0 1 2 3 4 5 6
My baby gets rashes easily (prickly heat).	0 1 2 3 4 5 6

My baby perspires a great deal.	0 1 2 3 4 5 6
My baby is very fond of cold foods and liquids (such as ice cream, cold juice, or ice water).	0 1 2 3 4 5 6
My baby gets overheated easily.	0 1 2 3 4 5 6
My baby gets irritable if a meal is delayed.	0 1 2 3 4 5 6
My baby gets irritable when hot.	0 1 2 3 4 5 6
My baby has a strong, full pulse.	0 1 2 3 4 5 6
My baby has warm hands.	0 1 2 3 4 5 6
My baby has light, fine hair (usually blond or red).	0 1 2 3 4 5 6
My baby prefers cool, ventilated places.	0 1 2 3 4 5 6
My baby is medium-boned with a medium build.	0 1 2 3 4 5 6
My baby has intense moods, slow in changing.	0 1 2 3 4 5 6
My baby has a moderate weight with good muscle tone.	0 1 2 3 4 5 6
My baby dislikes the sun.	0 1 2 3 4 5 6
My baby tends to be stubborn.	0 1 2 3 4 5 6
My baby becomes impatient more easily than other babies.	0 1 2 3 4 5 6

Add up your baby's Pitta points: _____

KAPHA							
My baby has a very calm, placid disposition.	0	1	2	3	4	5	6
My baby has a stuffy nose and a great deal of congestion.	0	1	2	3	4	5	6
My baby sleeps deeply and soundly.	0	1	2	3	4	5	6
My baby isn't happy in cool weather.	0	1	2	3	4	5	6
My baby tends toward plumpness.	0	1	2	3	4	5	6
My baby is a slow eater.	0	1	2	3	4	5	6
My baby's hair tends to be dark, thick, and wavy.	0	1	2	3	4	5	6
My baby rarely gets angry and seems to have no temper.	0	1	2	3	4	5	6
My baby is cuddly, even tempered, and good-natured.	0	1	2	3	4	5	6
My baby isn't affected if a meal is delayed.	0	1	2	3	4	5	6
My baby has regular daily bowel movements, steady, thick, and heavy.	0	1	2	3	4	5	6
My baby does well in any climate except very humid.	0	1	2	3	4	5	6
My baby's skin is thick, cool, and well lubricated.	0	1	2	3	4	5	6
My baby likes routine.	0	1	2	3	4	5	6

My baby has a larger than average bone structure.	0 1 2 3 4 5 6
My baby is stubborn and doesn't change moods easily.	0 1 2 3 4 5 6
My baby loves the wind and sun.	0 1 2 3 4 5 6
My baby doesn't like damp weather.	0 1 2 3 4 5 6
My baby has difficulty waking up.	0 1 2 3 4 5 6
My baby is slow in actions.	0 1 2 3 4 5 6

Add up your baby's Kapha points: _____

The highest number of total points in a specific dosha indicates your baby's dominant dosha. If totals from two doshas are close, then your baby has two dominant doshas. Although very rare, it's possible for all three scores to be fairly equal. If this is the case, then your baby is a tri-dosha.

Vata-dominant babies startle easily. They're extremely sensitive to wet diapers, cool drafts, and noise. Their bowel movements are irregular. They require less sleep and tend to wake up easily. Their moods swing easily; one minute they can be laughing, and the next crying.

Pitta-dominant babies have hearty appetites and are easily frustrated, especially when they're hungry. They're prone to diaper rashes, prickly heat, and skin problems. They focus intently on objects; and as they get older, they're persistent in the task they're working on (putting shaped blocks in their respective holes, and so forth). They're sensitive to sun and light.

Kapha-dominant babies are extremely cuddly. They sleep longer, deeper, and often through the night. They're not disturbed easily by sound or light, and tend to have heavy, large bone structures. In fact, they put on weight easily and are usually chubby babies. They tend to be more reserved and have regular bowel movements.

Have you figured out which mind/body type your baby is yet? If you have, then you're probably beginning to understand why she reacts to certain things. It's easier to accept your baby for who she is when you know that this is the child's disposition from birth. You can't change these basic elements of your baby's constitution. So why not learn to work with them? Be assured that your baby and you'll be best served by doing so.

Doshas in Nature

One of the most interesting and helpful principles of Ayurveda is the appreciation of how the larger environment in which we live affects and also expresses the three doshas. Vata, Pitta, and Kapha are at play everywhere in nature: Plants and herbs have doshas, as do animals and minerals. Nature has rhythm that keeps it in balance. Every flower has a time and a season for its bloom; every seed has a gestation time for its growth. Likewise, the three doshas are manifest in the seasons. In his book *Perfect Health,* Deepak Chopra writes: "As with the rhythms of the day, there are master cycles matched to the doshas that run throughout the year. Our bodies automatically flow with these changes as long as we do not interfere."[2] Understanding the balance of our own bodies according to dosha principles helps us to expand these concepts to the seasons of the earth.

+ Kapha season begins in mid-March and ends in mid-June,

+ Pitta season begins in mid-June and ends in mid-October, and

+ Vata season begins in mid-October and ends in mid-March

Learning more about doshas in nature will help us keep balanced in our own rhythm. Dr. Chopra explains, "When a cold wind begins to blow, the Vata inside you responds, because it too is cold and dry, and moving. It senses that something akin to itself has begun to dominate the scene. Each dosha recognizes a particular kind of weather that brings it out, according to the principle of 'like speaks to like.'"[3]

Thus, the moist Kapha within us responds. When winter begins to melt down, yielding to the flow of rain and wind, the Kapha inside you is likely to develop a running nose and sinus problems. And when the days are hot, sticky, and humid, the Pitta in you'll be easily aggravated, and may break out with a heat rash or sun poisoning.

+++

"If you always remember the real nature of things, you get rid of misery and illness."

— Charaka

We can adjust to the dosha cycles of the seasons by following certain dietary recommendations that preserve balance. These seasonal routines are called *ritucharya* in

Ayurveda. They require a shift of emphasis in lifestyle, but don't interfere with the diet that pacifies your predominant dosha.

+ In Kapha season, a diet that's lighter and drier should be favored. Reducing oil during this season is also advisable. Dairy should be greatly reduced, if not eliminated entirely, because it aggravates Kapha. Eat more bitter, astringent, and pungent tastes; and less sweet, sour, and salty tastes.

+ In Pitta season a diet of cool food and drink is desirable. Don't overeat during this hot season, because it will aggravate Pitta. The digestional fires, called agni, are lower at this time; therefore, appetites decrease with good reason. Honor this natural change. Drink cool, but not iced, liquids to douse the internal digestive powers. Eat more sweet, bitter, and astringent tastes; and less sour, salty, and pungent ones.

+ In Vata season a diet of warm foods and drinks, and more oily and heavy foods with substance is best. Eat more than you do in the other seasons, and don't worry about it—a tendency to eat more in the winter is natural and tends to pacify Vata at this time. Eat more sweet, salty, and sour tastes in winter; eat less bitter, astringent, and pungent tastes.

If you or your baby's body type matches a season, then that's the season you should monitor most vigilantly. If you're Kapha-dominant, be mindful of these changes in spring. If you're Pitta-dominant, then be more vigilant in summer. Vata-dominant mind/body types have more fragile constitutions and should take care of themselves in winter as well as the beginnings of all the seasons.

In addition to the dosha seasons, there are also daily cycles of doshas. These manifest twice each day. The first cycle begins when the sun rises:

+ 5 A.M. to 10 A.M. is Kapha time;

+ 10 A.M. to 2 P.M. is Pitta time; and

+ 2 P.M. to 6 P.M. is Vata time.

The second cycle begins when the sun sets:

+ 6 P.M. to 10 P.M. is Kapha time;

+ 10 P.M. to 2 A.M. is Pitta time; and

+ 2 A.M. to 6A.M. is Vata time.

Waking up during Vata time (2 A.M. to 6 A.M.) ensures a day of vigorous energy, especially if you went to bed the previous night during Kapha time (6 P.M. to 10 P.M.). If you go to sleep during Kapha time, your sleep will be deeper and more relaxed. Patients with severe depression have been known to spark a new vitality when their sleep patterns have been altered using this plan. Positive results have been achieved when bedtime is as early as 6 P.M. and rising time is as early as 2 A.M.

Raising children today is very challenging. The best thing you can do is pay attention to these recommendations, but never obsess over them. This information about the doshas is designed to make your life with your new baby *easier,* not harder. The intention of this book is to help you, as a parent, tune in to your child's mind/body needs. Knowing your baby's mind/body type will help you keep your baby balanced and healthy by allowing you to incorporate the dosha nutrition and other important Ayurvedic recommendations into his or her life. By doing so, you'll be promoting harmony, and thus preventing disease. Remember, the immune system of balanced people helps them resist disease more effectively than those who are out of balance. As a parent, you're the one who can best help to keep your family in balance. With healthier children, your job as a parent will be that much easier, and the rewards that much greater.

Summary

+ Knowing your mind/body type, or dosha—and following the recommendations for your type—will help keep you balanced and subsequently healthy.

+ The three mind/body types are Vata, Pitta, and Kapha.

+ Everyone's body has all three mind/body types in varying degrees.

+ If your Vata is out of balance, stay on a regular schedule for eating and sleeping, eat warm foods, and moisten skin with regular self-body massage.

+ If your Pitta is out of balance, practice moderation, eat cool foods like ice cream, and take cold showers.

+ If your Kapha is out of balance, exercise regularly, eat spicy foods, and stay away from dairy products.

+ Know your baby's mind/body type so that you'll understand his or her needs.

✦ A Vata baby must have total silence and minimum light for restful sleep.

✦ A Pitta baby demands meals on time, a cooler environment, and a lot of food.

✦ A Kapha baby needs activity and stimulation, routine, and very little dairy foods.

✦ Vata, Pitta, and Kapha's characteristics apply to the time of year—a Vata season is cold and dry, a Pitta season is hot and humid, and a Kapha season is wet and damp.

✦✦✦ ✦✦✦

✦ ✦ ✦ ✦ ✦ ✦ ✦ ✦

CHAPTER 3

✦ ✦ ✦ ✦ ✦ ✦ ✦ ✦

Centering Time: Silent Moments and Transcending Through the Senses

"True silence is rest for the mind.
It is to the spirit what sleep is to the body,
nourishment and refreshment."

— William Penn

THE THIRD SECRET IS KNOWING HOW TO CENTER AND BALANCE YOURSELF. If you're well balanced and healthy, your baby will thrive during its creation. The best way to achieve such a tranquil state is through meditation.

There are many different forms of meditation—some are vocal and some are silent. A common one is to silently repeat a word called a *mantra,* a Sanskrit term that means "mind instrument." The vibrational sound of the mantra helps you quiet your mind and releases you from your normal thinking patterns.

Meditation doesn't require you to adhere to any particular philosophy, religion, or lifestyle. It's something each and every one of us can do for ourselves, by ourselves. The Reverend Leo McAllister—a Catholic priest and the pastor of Our Lady of the Assumption parish in

Sacramento, California—highly recommends the practice of meditation. When he was a chaplain to the Assembly of the California State Legislature, he wrote:

> I am writing to allay any fears, anxieties, or misconceptions which Catholics may have concerning the practice of transcendental meditation [one form of meditation in which a word or mantra is repeated silently]. It's not a religion or a religious practice. In no way does it conflict with a person's belief in God or in his church. It's a simple, natural technique whereby, through regular practice, one can rid oneself of the stresses of the mind and enjoy deep rest and relaxation. There are many benefits which result from regular practice. A person's relationship with God and the practices of one's faith should be enhanced, rather than diminished, by the use of Meditation. One becomes much more sensitive to the presence of God in our universe and the interdependence and harmony which He intended to exist between peoples and things.

When you make the decision to meditate, you'll want to choose a special spot in your home exclusively for this purpose. Enhance your special spot with flowers, incense, pillows, and/or a mat so that comfort and peace will prevail in this space; it will also remind you that you've reserved a time and place for restoring balance and serenity. One of my first meditation teachers told students to shower or bathe before meditation, and suggested wearing clothing made of natural fiber. Your body is your temple, and physical purity will add to the peacefulness of the moment.

My special spot is in my bedroom, where I've set up a meditation table in front of a window that has a view of the Pacific Ocean. When I first sit down in my chair, I gaze out the window and appreciate the beauty of the sea just four blocks away. I've also created my own ritual that quiets my mind: I take a few deep breaths, and light two candles and some incense before I begin my practice. It's comforting for me to repeat the same routine twice a day, every day.

In some traditions, meditation is practiced facing the east in the morning, to honor the sun; and facing the north after sunset, to honor the point of balance within your being. In my bedroom, that's not possible; therefore, I've chosen to face the west—the sunset vista. I've created my own space for my own creative meditation process, and to me this seems right. But you should find what feels right for you.

It's best to start with short meditations, about five minutes at a time, and expand them as you grow into the practice. Enjoy the routine and the new feelings that develop, but don't try to force anything; you'll experience bliss gradually and naturally. Slowly increase your meditations to 20 minutes. These quiet, calming sessions will encourage you to make meditation a lifelong process.

For many years I used only visualization and breath techniques until I learned the transcendental meditation (TM) program. Here, the idea is to use a mantra to help disengage from one's senses and connect with a universal consciousness. Since using TM, I've noticed that I have more focus, energy, and peace—it even seems to stir up my creative energy. In fact, I've seen some of the greatest benefits of the practice while writing this book. Every day before sitting down at my computer, I take 20 minutes to sit in meditation. This allows me to focus clearly on each chapter I write, one at a time, so that the task becomes a joy. Time flies by.

Meditation also promotes self-awareness and enables me to avoid overreacting to chaotic situations. For example, when I drive on a busy freeway, I now have the composure to remain free of stress and anxiety, rather than give in to the frustration around me. When I realize that I'm being pulled away from my center, I can simply focus on my mantra and go back to balance with ease. My responses to everyday irritations have become more positive, and I've found myself more proactive.

It wasn't always that way. I didn't start meditating until my sons were off to college and my daughter was in high school. Before that, I allowed the mundane details of life to overwhelm and control me. A typical day during my child-rearing years consisted of running all over town: driving to orthodontist appointments for one son, carpooling to my daughter's dance lessons, stopping at the library to research an article I was writing. Changing hats, changing directions, and changing schedules led to poor eating habits, traffic tickets, and endless snapping at my kids. I rarely took the time to really talk to them or stop to hear what they had to say. Had I known then about the benefits of meditation, I could have handled my children with calm strength—instead of spurts of frantic frustration.

I identify with mothers everywhere I go. At the doctor's office, I see a mother trying to quiet an 18-month-old son with an earache—while her 5-year-old daughter is asking incessant questions about the book she's trying to read. Constantly glancing at her watch, the obviously frazzled young mother attempts to remain in control of the situation. Then she loses it. It's clear to me that the straw that has broken the camel's back is the disapproving look another mother has given her. I think, *If only I could wave a wand and transform the stress in these women's faces to peace.* All it would take is the gift that meditation makes available to everyone—the ability to remain above the fray and deal with challenges in a calm way.

+++

"When you are immersed in doing without being centered, it feels like being away from home. And when you re-connect with being, even for a few, you know it immediately. You feel you are at home no matter where you are and what problem you face."

— Jon Kabat-Zinn, Ph.D.

Modern science has produced numerous studies comparing the various methods of meditation, and transcendental meditation has figured heavily into this research. Results show that although meditation in general reduces anxiety, the TM program produces a markedly greater physiological effect than ordinary "relaxation" meditation. A highly distinctive state of restful alertness during TM was identified throughout the research.

Scientific studies have shown that meditation has many physical benefits—it lowers blood pressure, therefore improving cardiovascular health; it helps people reduce their use of caffeine, tobacco, and alcohol, as well as prescribed and non-prescribed drugs; it improves job performance, job satisfaction, and relationships; and it lowers respiration, reduces oxygen consumption, and decreases metabolic rate, thereby reducing the symptoms of aging.

Mantra meditation can help one reach a state of *self-actualization*. According to eminent psychologist Abraham Maslow, self-actualization is the style of functioning enjoyed by highly creative and successful people who have characteristics of health, fulfillment, and a high level of maturity—as well as a greater openness to experience.

While TM is the best known form of mantra meditation in the West, primordial sound meditation (PSM) is also gaining popularity. In PSM, the meditator (through silent repetition of a mantra) produces sound vibrations that slowly and gradually lead the mind out of its normal thinking process to "pure awareness." In *Ageless Body, Timeless Mind,* Dr. Deepak Chopra writes, "Pure awareness exists in the gap between thoughts; it's the unchanging background against which all mental activity takes place. We would not ordinarily suspect that such a state exists because our minds are so preoccupied with the stream of thoughts, wishes, dreams, fantasies and sensations that fill waking consciousness."[1]

Dr. Chopra has researched ancient mantra meditations and features them in primordial sound meditation classes at his center in Carlsbad, California. A Sanskrit word corresponding to the meditator's date and time of birth becomes his or her mantra. In this way, each person's mantra is personalized and will resonate to one's own vibrational center.

+++

*"The center that I cannot find
is known to my unconscious mind."*

— W. H. Auden

Specific Effects of Meditation During Pregnancy

Sheri Smith, an internationally trained meditation instructor, says, "Basically the purpose for meditation is to prevent the nervous system from falling into deep fatigue. During pregnancy it's really vital that the mother keep her energy as high as possible. Low energy and fatigue start putting pressure on the system, resulting in toxins in the mother's body and through her to the baby."

A pregnant woman in today's high-stress world can make changes to enhance harmony, health, and well-being for herself as well as the child she's co-creating. Gail Perry, an entrepreneurial businesswoman, did just that. The pressures of raising a toddler, combined with an unexpected second pregnancy and a hectic business schedule, motivated her to rearrange some things. She moved her business environment from a corporate high-rise to a home office. She also changed her daily routine by incorporating the practice of TM twice daily.

I was very nauseated up through my fourth month of pregnancy. When I began taking meditation classes, my instructor helped me focus on alleviating the nausea, as well as the pain and discomfort I felt. It was great, because she'd have me place my hands on whatever area in my body felt uncomfortable and concentrate on it until it dissipated.

Meditation also helped me deal with stress and fatigue—I could do a 30-minute meditation and feel refreshed, rested, and able to continue working. Even though it may sound like a contradiction, it's very energizing and relaxing at the same time. I'm sure it affected how I dealt with Shawn, my two-year-old.

Barbara Manley Wheeler has taught meditation—as well as classes on Ayurveda practices, lifestyle, and nutrition—for many years. She recently shared some thoughts on pregnancy and meditation with me.

> *When I think of pregnancy and this new life growing within a mother's womb, I can't think of anything more blissful than being in a state of silence* [achieved during meditation]. *It's almost a oneness with the embryo-baby. The silence has to do with our inner self and our inner world, instead of the stressors of the exterior world.*
>
> *We're exposed to stressors in the exterior world all day long. We're already setting our babies up for stressful situations because of the way our environment is. A beautiful way to have union with your embryo-baby growing within you is by meditating twice a day. It's important to continue to meditate after the baby is born. While you feed the baby, meditate—feeding a baby is in a sense meditation. Just being in silence with your baby—no TV or radio— and being centered in that moment creates a bonding experience.*

It's also important for the father to meditate, for both parents need to include a centering time in their day. Sheri Smith says, "If both parents don't meditate, disharmony in the family can manifest in the home. Meditation releases pressures in life." Gary Delaney, the president of a computer software company in La Jolla, California, and the father of three children, is delighted by the far-reaching effects of meditation in his life. He's now well aware of how his ability to handle work stress positively impacts his home life. When he's more at ease, his entire family experiences greater harmony. He asserts, "Once you experience the benefits, you'll find time to do it. . . . There's no question that it helps me deal with stress-related issues, and I'm in a pretty high-stress business."

Joy Star is a British woman who has meditated for many years and continued the practice while she was pregnant with her daughter, Ayisha. In fact, Joy used meditation as a way to heal herself from a previous miscarriage.

> *I was living in Majorca, Spain, when I lost my twins five months into my pregnancy. I didn't go to a doctor or anyone to heal me—I healed myself by meditating every day. I'd just take my tea, tell my body everything was fine, and meditate. At first I didn't realize that I wanted to be healthy and ready for another baby. Then, by meditating over the next six months and eating really well, I got ready in a really conscious way to have this baby. I hadn't been centered enough the first time, and I wasn't going to let it [a miscarriage] happen again.*

Joy cherished her time in meditation throughout her pregnancy. Eventually, she delivered a beautiful baby girl. Their close relationship continues to thrive 19 years later—now Ayisha meditates along with her mother as well as by herself.

Diane Keer, a woman who meditated throughout her second pregnancy, tells this story:

> *I saw a big difference between my first and second pregnancies because I didn't meditate with my first child. My son is my second child, and he seems to be*

*much more bonded to me than my daughter. He and I
are very connected on many levels.*

*I meditated throughout my pregnancy—I stopped
in the hospital, but resumed when I was discharged.
When I came home, I started noticing a pattern with
my new baby. He could be fed and dry and put to
sleep, but as soon as I'd start to meditate, he would
awaken—as if he wanted to be with me. As he got
older, I noticed an amazing thing. He'd be down the
street playing with friends, but when I'd start to meditate in my room, he'd come right back home. I guess
he was so connected that he wanted to share meditation time—just as he'd done as an infant.*

This type of bonding is a very beautiful thing. Once
a child is born, the mother can meditate while holding
her infant against her chest. This way, the child doesn't
feel left out or separated. Eventually, as a toddler, your
child can sit beside you in silence. Kids are never too
young to appreciate quiet time—if established at an
early age, it will provide them with a lifetime pattern for
centering.

Centering Your Baby Through the Five Senses

Babies learn through their senses: sight, sound,
smell, touch, and taste. Positive sensory experiences
can increase a child's capacity for learning, resulting in
a highly developed, intelligent, artistic adult. Albert
Einstein believed in using *all* the senses and integrating
them into the learning process—some believe his
approach for exploring the world around him increased

the richness of his work and gave him a centered, focused outlook on life.

My nephew, Michael, was born at the end of his sixth month. My sister Francine faced many challenges with him, but due to her background as an occupational therapist, she was able to work with him through stimulating his senses. His hand-eye coordination was underdeveloped, so she explored many motor-sensory-therapy programs. To activate his sense of touch, she encouraged him to feel velvet, sand, and other distinctive textures. She also played with him; showed him pictures; took him to museums; and provided him with many forms of visual stimuli, such as light and dark contrasts of color. Today, Michael is a brilliant artist. His intellectual ability is considered genius level. It's apparent that Francine's diligent work with him in his early life contributed to his abilities.

By the same token, you have the opportunity to increase your baby's exposure to positive and rewarding sense experiences. Providing sensory-rich experiences for your baby requires addressing each sense separately at first, and then in combination as she grows. This kind of thoughtful stimulation of the senses expands and enriches the nerve cells in the brain and increases her learning ability.

Positive sense experiences can also help her focus, have more energy, and maintain calm. In other words, sensory-rich experiences will help your child become centered.

Babies don't need to meditate. They come to us from the Creator and are still close to that spiritual realm. As parents, we need to cultivate and preserve that divine connection by honoring our children's individual rhythms and personalities.

SILENCE IS THE MOST BASIC WAY TO CENTER YOURSELF AND YOUR BABY. Simply holding her against your chest, with her head next to your heart, provides a peaceful, centering experience. And taking a warm bath with your baby can settle her down: The soothing water, your steady heartbeat, and the tranquility of a quiet moment offer you both an opportunity to return to balance.

Learning to sit in silence is a beautiful way to separate from all the external noise in our world. It's important for an infant to learn about his environment through the senses, but she can also be overstimulated. Your role is to provide the space, time, and patience to help your young child integrate all the incoming sensory data.

My granddaughter, Shelby, has always watched her mother, Alisa, meditate. She knows this is "quiet time." Alisa started to include Shelby at the age of two and a half. Alisa sits on the living room floor with a lit candle and invites Shelby to be seated with her. She tells Shelby to think really good thoughts: "Think about things you like to play with, or things you like to do—but just think, and don't speak."

Shelby loves to talk (which is typical for her age), but when she sits with Alisa, she quiets herself. Sometimes she whispers some of her favorite things ("Barbie . . . Baby Ozzy [her new kitten] . . . Mommy . . ."), but that's okay. A two-year-old just isn't old enough to understand the concept of *silent* meditation. However, it's never too soon to benefit from sitting quietly and whispering "good thoughts." It's a beginning.

Another way Alisa calms Shelby is by teaching her deep breathing. Shelby sits and takes deep breaths—but on occasion she'll snort, which leads to giggles. My granddaughter and daughter-in-law haven't perfected their meditation routine, but they're off to a good start. Maharishi Mahesh Yogi says that a child can't truly begin to meditate until he or she is old enough to keep a secret. At that time, children can be given their own mantra to keep to themselves. Until she reaches that point, Shelby is benefiting from the example of quiet time and the inward process of meditation as a normal, accepted part of every-day living.

Nature offers one of the best ways for children of all ages to increase their spiritual awareness and ability to center. Nature is rich and silent in comparison to the world of human activity. Through nature, a child experiences the vast peace of a blue sky. Allowing time for the child to savor the moment is a way of nurturing the child's connection with his inner spirit.

If a child is in a meadow and sees a beautiful fruit tree, she will run to it. On the way, if a dog appears between the tree and the child, the tree will be forgotten, and the furry animal friend will be all that exists to the child. Then the child may turn from the dog to a duck that happens to waddle by. With each encounter, valuable learning takes place—learning that we can't duplicate in the classroom or on a TV screen. It's the experience of being part of the har-mony of the natural world that imprints our memory with an awareness. Nature provides spiritual awareness for some, and for others it offers a place to go to when they want to be calm, quiet, and in balance.

RHYTHM IS THE SECOND WAY TO CENTER. Nature is rhythmic. The sun rises and sets; the seasons come regularly; the moon waxes to fullness and wanes to a void. Our lives take on a rhythm instinctively, such as natural sleeping and eat-ing patterns and menstrual cycles. In certain parts of the day or times of the year, our bodies feels more energized than at others. If you kept a chart of your rhythms, you'd probably find a pattern. Each of us has a unique bio-rhythm. In Chapter 2, I wrote about times of the day and year that are better suited to each dosha. Understanding this concept of cycles or rhythms will help you better understand your baby.

Babies take on their mothers' heartbeat rhythms when they're in the womb. Mothers who meditate are teaching their children about centering, even while their babies are still in the creative stages of fetal growth, through the gentle rhythms of their bodies. If a mother learns how to be centered herself, her embryo-baby will experience this same harmony. If a mother is uncentered and exemplifies frenetic, erratic energy, then her baby will have a more difficult time learning the attributes of balanced energy.

To understand rhythm is to understand polarity—fast and slow, active and passive, high and low. When your baby is experiencing an extreme rhythm, try bringing her back to a balanced rhythm by slowly working toward the opposite end of the spectrum. If an infant learns this behavior modification exercise early in life, it will serve as an excellent tool for her to modify her own behavior as she grows up.

For example, if your child is having a tantrum, you might try patting her back to the rhythm of her cries and screams. The emotion is frantic during a tantrum, so you must pat her in an equally frantic way. Match her rhythm and then slow down a little. She'll match your slower rhythm without even realizing it. Little by little, continue to slow down your strokes—soon she'll follow your lead and quiet down completely. As your child calms down and matches your slowing rhythms, you hold her attention for that moment.

Every child has three basic rhythms: *passive* rhythm, when she isn't active at all; *active normal* rhythm; and *excited* rhythm. Sometimes your child's rhythm gets out of control, such as when she becomes too excited, or too lethargic and passive. You must learn to pay attention and learn her rhythms. According to the Sufi teacher Inayat Khan, in his book *Education: From Before Birth to Maturity,*

> In order to understand the meaning of an infant's laughter and cry one must become an infant, because it's a language of another sphere. But when a person doesn't trouble about it, then its cry is only a nuisance and its laughter is a game. Sometimes people try and make the infant laugh more and more because they're interested or as an entertainment; or people neglect the infant, leaving it to cry and cry. Or the mother says, 'Be quiet, be quiet.' In all these cases they lose the opportunity of understanding the language of the infant.[2]

A parent only needs to pay attention and look a child in the eyes to get the message. We must have patience to learn this; once we do, we can have more success in centering our children.

Another way to center with rhythm is through music. One audio program that's good for centering infants is *Sounds of the Womb: Perfect Pacifiers.* Listening to music that's circular, like "Row, Row, Row Your Boat," and just hearing the repetitious melody is enough to grab a child's attention. Nursery rhymes are like that, too—and the rhythm of a rhyme is easy to remember. They always seem to put a smile on a child's face.

An ancient Vedic musical tradition uses sound, melodies, and rhythm to neutralize stress in the atmosphere. The music, called *Gandharva-Veda,* creates a harmonizing and balancing influence. Natural sound frequencies were so well understood by the ancient musicians that they were able to create musical compositions that mirrored the changing rhythms in nature.

Music tailored to the various mind/body types are very helpful for centering and for sleep. Vata music is relaxing and has an even rhythm, such as: "Rock-a-Bye Baby," and "Om Namaha Shivaya" (an ancient, smooth chant recorded by Robert Gass). Pitta music has a moderate beat with a light tempo and many high-pitched tones, like those in "Jingle Bells" and some of the songs from *West Side Story* ("I Feel Pretty" and "Something's Coming"). These songs ease the stress of an intense Pitta and replaces it with calm. Kapha music has a passionate, upbeat tempo to stimulate and invigorate the slow, calm Kapha.

In fact, drum music—even marches—are energizing for those with a Kapha dosha. Listen to Paul Simon's album *The Rhythm of the Saints,* or some of John Phillip Souza's marches to experience Kapha music. There are CDs and tapes out on the market today with music specifically made for Vata, Pitta, or Kapha constitutions. Musicians Bruce and Brian BecVar have recorded a set of three albums, entitled *The Magic of Healing Music,* for Deepak Chopra. Each album corresponds to one of the doshas. Babies love rhythm, and playing the right music is an excellent way to promote centering.

Understanding the doshas will help you select the

right music for your baby. But also pay attention to your child—notice how she responds to different musical beats. Make sure you're not making your Vata baby overexcited with Kapha music, or she'll have a hard time falling asleep.

AROMAS ARE THE THIRD DELIGHTFUL WAY TO CENTER. Essential oils are concentrated aromatic liquid substances that are extracted from flowers, trees, fruits, leaves, grasses, and roots. Before purchasing any oils, check with your health-food store. You'll want to make sure to get the proper oil for your needs. Of the many books on the subject, I recommend *The Complete Book of Essential Oils and Aromatherapy,* by Valerie Ann Worwood. Studies done in England verify the medicinal properties of aromatic essential oils, which include the following:

+ Leaves and twigs from the cinnamon tree help with flu, rheumatism, and warts—but avoid when pregnant. They're safe to use postpartum.

+ The flowering tops of the herb clary-sage help nerves and depression, and can calm a sore throat and other aches and pains. Don't confuse sage with clary-sage. Sage can be harmful to the baby.

+ The flowering buds of the clove tree help reduce nausea, flatulence, toothaches, and more. Avoid when pregnant, but savor in postpartum.

+ The flowering top of the lavender plant stimulates circulation, calms, promotes healing of open wounds, and can be used as an antiseptic. When pregnant, use it in concentrations of one percent or less.

+ The leaves and twigs of the neroli tree (orange blossom) work on the nervous system, releasing a calming effect; neroli facilitates easy breathing and increases the oxygen supply to the blood and brain. When pregnant, use in concentrations of one percent or less.

+ The seed from the *nutmeg tree* is an analgesic; and it reduce insomnia, nervousness, nausea, and vomiting. When pregnant, use in concentrations of one percent or less.

+ The flowers and petals from the *rose bush* are a uterine relaxant. They help ligaments to soften, enabling the pelvic bones to expand; and also eases circulatory problems.

These essential oils are convenient and versatile to use. Extracted from specific species of plant life, these complex, precious liquids help balance us emotionally and physically. They provide pleasure and protection, and can be used as healing remedies and centering tools.

The brain's limbic system processes emotions. An odor message goes directly to the limbic system, which is why aromas can affect our mood. The odor's message then moves onward to the *hippocampus,* the area of the brain responsible for memory. The essences create memory cells—forming a memory perception. That's why smells can bring back specific memories: the joys of our grandmother's garden, the comfort of homemade bread being baked on a cold winter day, or the laughter of a fifth-grade teacher who wore a certain perfume.

Scent is very powerful and can elicit emotions. Certain aromas can calm and relax, while others can stimulate. A child's sensory perception is much keener than an adult's, so the dosage of essential oils for children should be half the amount of an adult dose. Additionally, "less is more" is the best approach when creating a blend. Be especially careful when using oils with newborns; even one drop of oil can be too much.

There are different methods of working with aroma oil. You can rub it on your body, letting it absorb through your skin; or you can inhale it through your nose, inhalation purifies the lungs and can enhance moods. You can put the scent on a cotton ball under your nose, but the preferred way to inhale essences is by using a diffuser. Diffusers are simply containers of warm water used to heat oils, allowing their molecules to release into the atmosphere. It's important that the surface of the bowl or pot you use isn't porous, so it can be wiped clean for future use with a different oil. To prevent essences from overwhelming a room and getting into your baby's mucous membranes or eyes, it's important to diffuse the oils with water: Heat a pint of water until steaming and place one drop or less of oil in the water. Place the water in your child's room, away from your baby's head.

Parents can also use oils for baby massage (see Chapter 4). Lavender is especially relaxing and can be easily mixed with sesame oil.

Robin Gunning, a mother and aromatherapy student, has personally experienced the effects of scent with her little girl.

I've been using the essential oils ever since my daughter, Margo, was born. She's now three years old, and a living example of how emotional and physical imbalances can be brought to balance through essential oils. I've used Roman chamomile a great deal with Margo for centering. [Roman chamomile oil is very uplifting and promotes a blissful feeling. Robin uses it for massage and any time she and her daughter sit and have a quiet time.]

Margo had a skin condition, a little rash that I felt was related to something that made her nervous. So I used citrus to balance her emotions [rashes are usually a Pitta imbalance; therefore, Robin was balancing Margo's dosha with this oil]. *Children resonate well to citrus. They really like the smell of tangerine and mandarin. I used bergamot* [the peel from the fruit of the bergamot tree is good for acne and fevers] *to help her skin condition, and that also has a citrus aroma. I added a little bit of lavender in it to soothe and calm her. I used the blend to rub on her skin, and she healed naturally.*

When my daughter was born, she and I were separated for about 15 days. I was in the hospital and she went home. The woman who was taking care of her felt that Margo was stressed from our separation. She felt Margo needed grounding, and eventually she decided to put neroli and chamomile oils all over my baby. Neroli had a calming effect on Margo, and for the first time, she slept through the night.

Oils can also benefit mothers. For a pregnant woman, the application or inhalation of essential oils can help harmonize the emotional, physical, and spiritual. They relax cramped legs and relieve nausea. It's ideal to seek that harmony and unity because when a mother is going through the stressful transitions of pregnancy, her unborn embryo-child is affected. "On the emotional sphere," aromatherapy specialist Rodney Schwan told me in an interview in April of 1995, "one can integrate the oils with meditation for centering and balance, to enhance the state of bliss. The embryo-child is affected by the scent the mother is using; therefore, the mother must be very careful when selecting the proper scent during pregnancy."

Because aromas have a major influence on the embryo-child while in the womb and later, you'll want to use gentler oils—such as spearmint instead of peppermint. Find out which oils in the same family are the mildest.

The skin goes through a tightening sensation in pregnancy. Jasmine can have a softening effect. For a pregnant mother, gently rubbing jasmine oil on her tummy not only has a regenerative effect on the skin (preventing stretch marks), but it can also have an antidepressant effect, uplifting the mother-to-be's spirits. It balances through the hypothalamus gland and sends endorphins to the nerve cells. The baby will get the pleasant endorphin rush just as the mother does.

Other oils can positively affect the pregnant mother. Some to try are:

Geranium	Lavender	Rose maroc
Grapefruit	Mandarin	Tangerine
Jasmine	Rose bulgar	Ylang-ylang

These oils can be used in the shower or bath, or added to a massage oil. They can also be used in aromatic diffusers and on electric bulbs. Heating the oil allows molecules to be released into the atmosphere. It's important when pregnant to remember to always use minimum quantities.

The benefits of essential oils to both mother and child are innumerable. However, essences need to be used selectively and under the guidance of a licensed aromatherapy practitioner so that proportions and strengths can be adjusted properly. According to Robert Tisserand, author of *The Art of Aromatherapy* and publisher of *The International Journal of Aromatherapy,* there are many essential oils that must be avoided when pregnant. In his *Safety Data Manual,* he warns pregnant women of the dangers of the following essential oils and aromas: basil, cinnamon, clove, fennel, hyssop, marjoram, myrrh, origanum, sage, savory, tarragon, and thyme.

Other essential oils to avoid are:

Bitter almond	Mugwort	Tansy
Boldoleaf	Mustard	Thuja
Calamus	Pennyroyal	Wintergreen
Camphor,	Rue	Wormseed
yellow	Sassafras	Wormwood
Horseradish	Savin	
Jaborandi leaf	Southernwood	

Pregnant women should only use the following essential oils in concentrations of one percent or less:

Chamomile	Citrus	Lavender
Geranium	Frankincense	Sandalwood
Rose		

COLOR AND LIGHT ARE THE FOURTH WAY TO CENTER. In Ayurveda, the three doshas are associated with colors and specific hues. The Vata baby likes relaxing greens or quiet pinks. The Pitta needs cooling and calming hues, such as blue. Kaphas benefit from a little activity—and hot pink or red are the most vibrant colors. Doshas should be taken into consideration when painting your baby's room.

Light causes emotional responses in humans that can disrupt balance, depending on its intensity and its color vibration. Infants and toddlers display more marked responses to light than older children and adults, as their eyes are less accustomed to the vibrations of light (in the womb, the baby's environment is dark and cozy).

As you come to understand how light affects your baby, you may want to install a dimmer switch on the light in your baby's room. Some children feel secure in a darkened room. Conversely, if a room is too dark, it will upset some children. A dimmer allows you to adjust the light according to your child's preference; as your child grows and his response to light changes, you can continue to make adjustments.

THERE ARE MANY THINGS WE CAN DO TO BALANCE our babies and small children, but first and foremost, the mother and father need to be centered. In the womb, your baby's environment must be healthy and harmonious in order for the baby to thrive; therefore, during pregnancy, you need to keep your body in optimal condition. Your child will pick up even the most subtle energy exchanges in her environment.

Once your child is born, the benefit of taking the time to center yourself will be reflected in the overall harmony of your family. When you get home from work, take time out before rushing into activities. Let the entire family share the time-out session—call it the centering moment or quiet time. If you start early with these types of centering practices, they'll become second nature to your children. You may find your regular silence time a wonderful bonding experience for your whole family.

Summary

+ A balanced, centered mother helps produce a balanced, centered baby.

+ A meditation spot is a sanctuary, and it communicates a special message to your inner mind: that you have set aside time and space to center yourself.

+ Meditation prevents the nervous system from falling into deep fatigue.

+ Babies don't need to meditate, but do they need positive sense stimulation. Silence is the most basic way to balance yourself and your baby.

+ Rhythm, aroma, and colors are all delightful ways to soothe and center yourself and your baby at the same time.

+++   +++

+ + + + + + + +

CHAPTER 4

+ + + + + + + +

Touch Time:
Massage for Your Baby and You

*"Being touched and caressed,
being massaged, is food for the infant.
Food as necessary as minerals,
vitamins, and proteins."*

— Dr. Frederick Leboyer

THE FOURTH SECRET IS TOUCHING. The human fetus, when less than eight weeks old, can feel a touch—in fact, it's the first sense developed. Your touch is the first form of stimulation that your baby will perceive. Sound will be the next sense developed in the womb—but before your baby develops auditory faculties, she'll be able to *feel* the vibrational tones of your voice. Sound touches the embryo through vibration; therefore, you can sing and talk to your baby from the beginning of your pregnancy.

A baby's first massage is given by nature long before birth. The gentle rocking and floating that begins soon after conception becomes a soft caressing by the womb. Surrounded by fluid, the embryo moves to the rhythm of the mother. As the embryo grows, the womb is less roomy and the baby floats less; the mild, pulsating, oscillating motion begins squeezing the baby. The constant stimulation of the womb continues to increase as the baby grows larger and has less space to move around. Within this ideal physical environment, the developing baby is being touched all the time.

When the mother is in conscious contact with the baby, the harmony of the baby's in-utero experience can be enhanced even more. However, as Monica Ward, a certified baby massage therapist, once told me: "Unfortunately, many times mothers don't even tune in to the rhythm of their babies inside them. They only tune in to how their body is responding to pregnancy."

As you adapt to the new life growing within, massage can be a wonderful way to feel your changing body in a positive, accepting way—as well as to tune in to the rhythms of your growing baby. Massage provides a wonderful way to get to know one another as you listen to the nuances of your body and to the responses of your baby within the walls of your womb. Massage slows you down so that you can be in the moment with your body and your baby. A caring touch can ease away the tension and stress that might cause your energy to be drained.

There are many advantages to massage during pregnancy, including relaxing tight muscles; relieving stress on your ankles, knees, and lower back; increasing circulation; reducing swelling; easing muscle strain in the back and neck; and giving you physical as well as emotional nurturing. Massage stimulates endorphins under the skin to give you more energy, and it assists the release of metabolic waste that can make you feel tired and listless. One of the greatest benefits of massage is that it can make you more aware of your body so you can then respond to your needs. The ultimate advantage of pregnant massage is that your baby benefits when *you* benefit.

Catherine E. Halmay, a holistic health practitioner, has had extensive experience providing massage therapy to pregnant women and infants. She's been involved in this aspect of massage since 1987, when she herself was pregnant. At that time, she was disappointed because she was unable to find competent massage therapists. She told me, "I knew how important massage was, but I had difficulty finding a therapist to give me a good massage when I was pregnant. It seemed that they weren't prepared to work with me being pregnant. For starters, they didn't even have the pillows to cushion my body for maximum comfort."

According to Catherine, the best way for an expectant mother to position herself for massage is to lie down on her side and support her body with pillows: one under her head, another between her knees, and the third enfolded gently between her arms and against her chest. If desired, a pillow can also be used to support her belly.

Pregnant Massage

The following instructions are addressed to the person giving the massage:

It's best for you to prepare for the massage by making sure the room is at a comfortable temperature and by warming the massage oil. Have the mother-to-be lie down on her side, and get pillows in place so that she's comfortable. Now position yourself behind the pregnant woman, with one hand on her shoulder to provide support. With your other hand, begin long, gliding movements from her hip, up to and then around her shoulder. As you repeat this elongated stroke, gradually increase the pressure. Cup your hand around the muscle at the top of her shoulder and gently squeeze. Tiny circular motions with your thumb at the edge of the shoulder blade, as well as larger circular movements with your palm, can help the tension release. Don't apply more pressure until you feel the muscles relax.

Small, circular movements can also be made on the long muscles that run on either side of her spine. Apply pressure alongside of the spine, but don't work on the spine itself because its integral nervous system is delicate (leave this sensitive area to a professional masseuse who's studied anatomy and knows techniques suitable for the spine). Move your strokes up to her neck, gently applying pressure. Now work your way down—from neck to hip. The neck and hips are the most important areas to work when massaging the back because the weight and pressure of the belly at the front of the body pulls specifically on these muscles.

Once you've thoroughly worked one side of the mother, remove the pillows, gently help the mother turn, replace the pillows, and begin on her other side with the same massage sequence.

Another beneficial massage can be done with the pregnant woman straddling a chair backwards with a pillow cushioning her head and chest. Kneel behind her for the best leverage. Have her lean into the pillow with her head, and knead the muscles immediately around her *sacrum* (triangular-shaped, lower-back area) with your thumbs. Continue with elongated strokes up along either side of her spine. This mini-massage can be a great release for her lower back.

Even as little as 15 minutes a day can relieve much of the discomfort of back pain during pregnancy. Massage is sensuous, and it makes you feel relaxed and refreshed. Don't forget: When you feel good, your baby feels good; when your body is relaxed, your baby feels the endorphins of relaxation; when you nurture yourself, you also nurture your baby.

Self-Massage

Self-massage is also very beneficial because it puts you more in touch with your body. Sometimes we're so busy that we ignore our bodies altogether! The daily practice of self-massage (abhyanga) is recommended by Ayurvedic practitioners for everyone, pregnant or not. It assists in promoting more flexibility in the joints, muscles, and tissues; and also helps to lubricate the skin, giving it more luster and youthfulness. By stimulating the skin and hormones under the skin, the body's natural pharmacy releases endorphins that promote a feeling of well-being.

In order to prepare for your self-massage, you'll need a quarter cup of warm sesame oil, which you can purchase in a health-food store. Refined sesame oil is recommended because it's lighter (don't use the Chinese sesame oil— it's prepared differently and is heavier with a stronger scent). Warm your oil in the microwave for 10 to 15 seconds, or set a plastic container of oil in hot water until it reaches body temperature. I recommend that you do your massage in the bathroom because it can be messy. It's best to be seated for this massage, so you'll need a small stool or chair.

Once seated, pour a tablespoonful of the warm oil

into the palm of your hand. Rub into your scalp, moving your palm in circular strokes around your entire head. Proceed to your ears and neck, using a more gentle touch, and then move to the temples.

Continue massaging your neck and shoulders. Pour more oil into your palms as needed, and progress to your arms, using long strokes back and forth. When you reach your elbows and shoulders, change to a more vigorous circular stroke. As you come to the trunk of your body, slow down. With a slow, circular, clockwise motion, massage your chest and belly. The embryo in the womb feels your hands as you stroke your belly—touch serves as a bridge between the fetus and the outside world.

Now reach around to your lower back; without straining, massage in an up-and-down motion. Then, along your legs, use long strokes back and forth. The knees and hip joints should be massaged with hands moving in a circular, clockwise direction. Finally, pour the remaining oil on your feet and give them a vigorous massage with the flat of your hand, using your fingers to stimulate your toes.

After the massage, you'll want to bathe and wash your hair. Put shampoo directly on your hair before you add water; this will remove the oil more easily than if you wet your hair first. Use mild soap and warm water for bathing the rest of your body. A small, undetectable amount of oil may stay on your skin, which is beneficial because it assists in keeping your muscles warm and your skin moist.

Self-massage is a wonderful way to start your day because it wakes up your body. I've gotten in the habit of doing this every day, and it truly makes a difference in my life. I feel more energized and my skin glows with health.

The Benefit of Baby Massage

Remember, massage benefits both you and your unborn child—every time you get a massage, your baby gets one, too. During birth, labor contractions stimulate the neuropeptides beneath your baby's skin, which send the signal to the respiratory system that it's time to get ready to breathe. The friction your baby feels from gradually being pushed down through the birth canal acts as a full-body massage, stimulating her organs to start working on their own. In a longer labor, your baby has more opportunity to prepare herself for life outside the womb.

C-section babies don't receive this stimulation from the birth canal. Consequently, they can benefit greatly from massage, which will help replace some of the stimulation they didn't receive.

Massage is also therapeutic to your baby after she's born. You may find that you constantly want to touch your new baby—this is natural. The touching confirms that your baby really has arrived, and it reestablishes the bond you experienced before you gave birth—making your baby feel nurtured and secure as you apply rhythmic stimulation and touch, reminiscent of the natural massaging of the womb.

Studies have shown that infants thrive when touched frequently. A research study on premature babies conducted by psychologist Tiffany Field, director of the Touch Research Institute at the University of Miami School of Medicine in Florida, demonstrated that daily massage is of tremendous benefit. Premature infants massaged three times per day, 15 minutes at a time, gained 47 percent more weight than babies not massaged. The study also found that the massaged babies were more active and alert, and their average hospital stay was six days less than that of the nonmassaged premature babies. Further, the babies who received massage therapy matured neurologically at a more rapid pace than those who didn't.

The long-lasting effects of touch are just beginning to be understood. In Cleveland, Ohio, a study conducted at the Rainbow Babies and Children's Hospital suggested that language and reading skills, as well as IQ, were enhanced in children who had the benefit of loving touch from an early age. More studies are under way to determine the extent of the effect of touch on babies' health and growth. At the very least, we know that babies need touch to survive and thrive.

+++

"Holding contains the invisible threads
that tie us to our existence.
From the first moments of our life to the last,
we need to be held—or we fall."

— Ruthellen Josselson, Ph.D.

It's essential to have tactile stimulation to adequately develop organically and psychologically. According to anthropologist Ashley Montagu, the first communication an infant gets is through skin sensation. Animals lick their young to stimulate them to fully develop; human touch and massage act in the same way with human babies.

Each of the nerves in the body is covered by fatty tissue called the *myelin sheath.* This covering acts as insulation, protecting the nerve from damage—but it isn't completely formed at birth. Massage sends signals to the brain to promote accelerated growth of the myelin sheath.

Massage also teaches the baby how to relax—improving respiration and circulation. Each cell receives more oxygen when circulation increases, thus allowing more flexibility in the feet and hands. Sleep patterns become stabilized, and babies are able to resist disease.

Barbara Manley Wheeler has been teaching self-massage (abhyanga) and other healthy mind/body practices to her patients for quite some time. She feels very strongly about the tangible health benefits of massage for both mothers and infants:

> *It's very important to continue abhyanga after the baby's birth because it will help you get back in balance. It wakes up the hormones in the internal pharmacy within our body; it stimulates the skin, which in turn stimulates and creates the neuropeptides. To use the abhyanga technique on your baby would be the most loving, nurturing, and stimulating thing you could do for him or her. Massage is also beneficial to babies because it helps develop strong immune systems to fight off the little viruses they may come in contact with.*

Baby massage can begin as soon as the umbilical cord falls off. Until then, it's best to swaddle the infant with a blanket wrapped snugly around her body. This can help make her feel secure even when you aren't holding her. Coming out into this world can be a shock to your baby's system. Swaddling is a common practice in many cultures around the world because it simulates the warm feeling of the womb.

With a newborn, massage must be done with a very light touch—avoiding the navel area so it can heal. It's best performed slowly, as you'll be getting to know and learn about your baby through your hands. Also, babies respond to massage differently than adults do. Adults relax even when a tense spot is touched and it hurts, because our bodies know that we can work through the pain to release the tension. Infants are a little wary, because massage is something very new to them; they don't understand that if there is an area in their body that hurts, the pain can be relieved. They only know that there is pain or pleasure.

Each baby is very individual—and when parents take the time to quiet down their own energies, they can tune in to their baby's subtle preferences. It's important for parents to learn the level of touch their baby needs. Let your baby teach you what to do, and trust your intuition.

+ + +

"Parents learn not only to know their child,
his body and all his characteristics, reactions,
and expressions, but they also become aware
of their own particular way of touching their
child, of pacifying him and of holding him
so he feels safe and secure."

— Tina Heinl

Monica Ward, a massage therapist who specializes in baby massage, says that she asks parents to make observations about their baby and write them down in a notebook. Noticing if your baby is more visual, auditory, or kinesthetic (touch-oriented) can help you understand your baby's needs during massage.

Infants need a balance when you massage them. Energy currents go up and down the body—going up the body is more stimulating, and going down is more calming. At times you'll need to do some stimulation to excite your baby, or you may need to stroke downward to calm her. A child who is more active and excited needs a more gentle and grounded massage—a slow-moving baby will need a touch that's more active. (This is a good time to refer back to the baby dosha questionnaire in Chapter 2.)

If your baby has a dominant Vata mind/body type, she's sensitive to light and noise. Therefore, prepare the environment by dimming the lights, closing the shades, and making sure there's no TV or radio blaring in the next room. Since Vata babies are uncomfortable if they're chilled, make sure that the room is nice and warm.

A very important consideration is your baby's temperament. Under normal conditions, Vata babies tend to be stimulated easily, are physically active, and have trouble settling down to sleep. Remember this when massaging your Vata baby: Slow massage soothes her, getting her into a slower rhythm so she'll calm down. This is a wonderful way to ready her for sleep time.

The Pitta-dominant baby gets overheated easily and is irritable if she's too hot. Prepare her environment by making sure that the room is well ventilated and on the cool side. If it's summer, place a fan in the corner of the room away from the baby. Watch for signs of impatience from your Pitta child, because if she's getting restless, you may need to pick up the speed of your massage. You never want to give a fast massage—yet if you're going too slow, a Pitta baby may find the pace irritating. Don't give up trying to please her. She'll direct you to the right rhythm and the right touch. *Moderation* is the key word with Pittas.

The Kapha baby can be described as calm, placid, even slow-moving—and needs to be stimulated. A more vigorous, active touch will wake up the Kapha-dominant baby. Since Kaphas are sound sleepers but have difficulty waking up, you may want to give a massage in the morning. If mornings are agreeable to your baby, then make it a daily habit—Kaphas love routine. Kaphas are disagreeable in humid and damp weather, so a dehumidifier is recommended when necessary.

As you can see, Ayurveda gives you an advantage when interpreting the signals your baby send to you. "When we truly listen to our infants we are fulfilling all their psychological needs," says Vimala Schneider McClure in *Infant Massage.*[1]

By knowing your baby's mind/body type, you'll be able to understand your baby and respond accordingly.

SOME BABIES SNUGGLE AND CUDDLE (USUALLY KAPHAS); they're definitely "touchers" and will always be touchers. Other babies turn away when cuddled or snuggled; they respond better to words and love to be talked to and read to. They're "nontouchers." When kids who are nontouchers are raised in an environment where there are a lot of physical displays of affection, they don't feel loved—they feel smothered. Likewise, touchers raised by parents who are nontouchers tend to feel neglected because they aren't cuddled as much.

It's not uncommon for kids who need more physical attention become accident-prone to get kind affection they desire. This is vital information for adults because it underscores the importance of learning to "read" our children so that we can communicate well with them. Identifying if your child is a toucher or nontoucher early in life will help you know how often your child wants a massage—or if she even wants one at all.

When I was raising my daughter, Angie, I wasn't aware of the toucher/nontoucher theory. Her older brothers had loved to be cuddled, massaged, and touched. She, however, was always pushing me away. I now realize that she was on the other end of the touch spectrum. At the time, I didn't know how to respond to what I perceived as her cool attitude. I felt that she had never bonded with me, and I interpreted her dislike for touch as rejection or mistrust. Since becoming aware of the toucher/nontoucher approach to relationship communication, I've realized that she would have preferred me to read to her or converse with her with more often. She's now 22—a lovely young woman—and I finally understand how to relate to her.

Tuning in to your toddler's innate communication preferences can prevent future misunderstandings. Asking a toddler where she's hurting, when did she first feel badly, and so on, helps her learn to pay attention to her body's signals. If your child is a toucher, adding a gentle touch during your questioning can evoke a more heartfelt response. Touches of reassurance that demonstrate love are very important to add to time spent communicating with your youngster—provided she is a toucher. Children who are nontouchers will appreciate the time you spend reading to them or playing games with them more than anything else.

Massaging Your Baby

Before you begin the massage, rub the palms of your hands together. Then slowly separate them and feel the energy field between your palms. How far apart are your palms before the energy fades? This is important to note, because your baby also has an energy field surrounding her. She can feel your proximity before your hand actually comes in contact with her skin. The best way to begin a massage on a new baby is to slowly move the palms of your hands over the baby's energy field. This will serve as an introduction to the massage that will follow.

The environment where you conduct the massage and the time you select are of special importance. A bathroom is an ideal area in which to massage the infant because the temperature can be easily regulated; it's also recommended that a bath follow the baby massage.

The massage itself takes only five or ten minutes to give, but you'll need to set aside extra time for preparation. You'll need several items for massage/bath time: You'll need three large bath towels, a baby bathtub filled with extra-warm water (water will cool while you massage), a baby washcloth, warm sesame oil (see "Self-Massage" earlier in this chapter), and perhaps one or two pillows covered in plastic. Make sure your nails are smooth and that you've removed all your jewelry to prevent scratching the baby.

Spread out a large towel near the bathtub, and put the oil bottle in hot water to keep it warm. Remove your shoes, and be sure that you're dressed so that your legs are bare (in order to have skin-to-skin contact during the entire massage). Remove your baby's clothing and diaper. Sitting comfortably—preferably with your back against

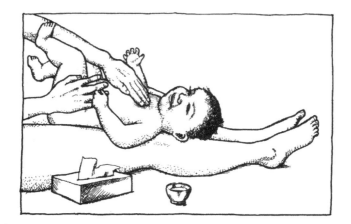

the tub for support, legs stretched out in front of you, using the pillows if necessary—you'll notice that your baby fits nicely on your lap with the back of her head on your knees. In this position, you can both look at each other. Take a few deep breaths. Breathe with your baby to establish harmony.

Tell yourself that love flows through you to your child. Pour the warm oil into your hands and show your palms to her. By looking into her eyes, ask permission to massage her. Although this may sound a bit odd at first, it's important to communicate your intention through visual contact before commencing. At first she may not understand what you're asking, but even a very young infant will catch on after the first few times. You'll quickly learn to recognize your baby's reactions; by observing her body language you'll know if the time is right. Asking your baby for consent shows her that you respect how she feels about being touched, and it teaches her to respect her body and feelings. This is an important concept to introduce at this time, because as she matures, your child will know that only she has the right to give permission to be touched.

Soon your baby will recognize the cue that massage time is to begin, and she'll respond with a grin, laugh, or wiggle. Smile, all the while telling your child that you love her. Your body will express your love through every movement. After a few massages, the baby will know what you're about to do by the sound of the oil moving in your hands and by the position she's in. If you make all the preparations and your baby reacts irritably or is tired, plan to do the massage at another time.

There are various ways to start the massage. Sensitive babies may be startled if you don't build up to the massage very slowly and gently, and some baby-massage practitioners believe that gently moving your hands above the baby before you touch the skin is a good warm-up procedure. Monica Ward (the baby massage practitioner mentioned earlier in this chapter) recommends starting with the head because you get to look into your baby's eyes and establish communication. Touching the head opens up the chakras (the energy points of the body, according to the ancient Vedic system) and allows you to continue eye contact.

Additionally, your baby's face may hold a great deal of tension accumulated from interaction with the world around her—from crying, teething, and sucking.

The head is very sensitive, so your touch must be extremely gentle and soothing. Begin with small circles around the top, sides, and back of the head. Massage your baby's ears softly, but avoid entering the ear. The forehead is next. With fingers from both hands centered on her forehead, stroke outward, toward the temples. Then go on to the sinus area, with your forefingers lightly stroking away from the center of your baby's face. Circle as gently as you can with your palms on her temples and cheeks. Re-oil your hands whenever needed, but avoid putting too much oil on her face. Use your thumb or forefinger to work around the baby's mouth and chin. Gently move to the chin with both hands, using your fingertips to pull up under the chin. As you sweep up the neck, front and back, you'll be relaxing her jaw and stimulating the little lymph nodes in this area. By now your baby is becoming calm.

As you massage a specific area of your child's body, such as the neck, repeat your motion three times before going on to the next area. The first time, you're introducing the movement; the second time, she recognizes the move and knows what to expect; the third repetition reinforces the memory of the movement.

After massaging her head, face, and neck, move down to her legs and feet. Stroke down your baby's body in a fluid motion without taking your hands off of her. Legs and feet can be the most pleasurable areas to receive massage. The feet have many nerve endings that link to other parts of the body, and massaging them can stimulate internal organs, prevent various imbalances, and relax muscles throughout your baby's body. Remember, her legs have been cramped in the fetal position for nine months. By the time she's crawling, your baby is really getting a workout in her legs, knees, and buttocks. Massage relieves tension and stretches out her muscles. Once you relax her feet and legs, she'll be mesmerized.

Gently press your thumb against the sole of your baby's foot. Move your thumb, pressing gently from heel to toe. Each little toe can be gently squeezed and wiggled. Hold her leg with both hands and gently move from the foot to the hip, turning and gently twisting in both directions. Complete your massage of one foot and leg, then proceed to the other side.

Now you'll begin massaging her chest, which helps

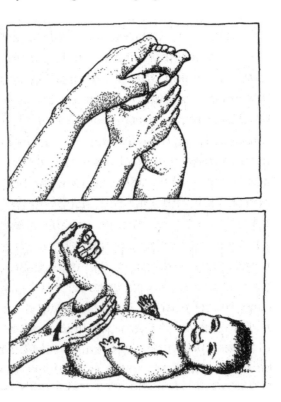

tone the lungs and heart. Sometimes babies close their arms around their chest to protect their vital organs. If this happens, use a technique borrowed from Aikido (one of the Japanese martial arts): Change the rhythm of your movements and blend with your baby's movements until she finally gives up resistance and relaxes. She'll soon come to love having her chest massaged.

Place your hands palms down on your baby's chest and push out to the sides as if you were smoothing the pages of a book. Sweep up her chest and out toward her arms with a fluid motion, using the tips of your fingers. Use just enough oil to avoid friction, but not enough to be too slippery. Bring your hands back around her torso to the center in a heart-shaped motion. Now, with your hands at the bottom of your baby's rib cage and extending to the sides, you're ready to move your hands, one at a time, across her chest in a diagonal sweep. Alternate hands and sweep up to the shoulders. Repeat three

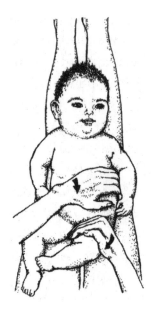

times in a rhythmic crisscrossing of the little torso.

The tummy massage is important for digestion and elimination purposes, and it's wonderful for releasing gas. Make sure that the umbilical cord is completely healed before massaging the stomach area. Pour some warm oil into the palms of your hands and then place your warm hands on your baby's tummy for a few moments. Move both hands at the same time in a semicircle around her navel in a clockwise direction, with your left hand above the navel and the right hand below the navel. Your baby may experience some discomfort at first, as gas bubbles may be released. However, this will soon pass, and she'll be very content with this tummy massage. If she's fidgety, it may mean that gas bubbles are still lodged in this area: Look at her and talk to her gently while holding her feet up against your belly. With your free hand, make a circle on her tummy, starting in the left corner. Her discomfort will subside. Colicky babies will especially benefit from this tummy massage.

Arms and hands are massaged next. Use a circular motion on the shoulder, then extend your baby's arm with one hand and massage in one long stroke with the other hand. Repeat this motion three times. Then, with both hands snugly around her arm, twist gently in both directions—using a kneading technique from her shoulder to the wrist and back again. With your thumb, make circular patterns in your baby's palm. Continue the circles on the back of her hand. Use circular motions on every joint, including the elbow. Use a straight back-and-forth movement on her upper arm. Next, holding her arm above her head, gently stroke your baby's armpit three times. This massages the lymph nodes. Repeat this entire routine with the opposite arm and hand.

Now turn your baby over so that she's on her tummy—facedown across your lap. A "hello" stroke from the top of her head to her toes is a nice way to begin. This can be the most relaxing part of the massage. Beginning with both palms together on the top of your baby's back, move your hands in opposite directions—out away from the spine. Repeat this stroke, each time moving farther down the back, all the way to the buttocks. Keeping the right hand secure at the buttocks, sweep the left hand down from the neck to meet the other hand. Continue down to the ankles; repeat three times. As you end the massage, lighten up on strokes, giving light nerve strokes from your baby's head down to her toes. Little muscles will begin to develop right under your fingers as she grows.

The most challenging part of baby massage is getting a good balance with your touch: not too fast or too slow, too firm or too soft. With newborns you have to work very slowly and gently, but as they get older (around five months), they actually like a firmer touch. You'll get over your awkwardness and, after a while, will automatically know what touch your child needs.

This is such a beautiful experience for parents and baby, because you're both equally present in the moment. You're showing love and respect, and you're teaching caring. You're also helping the baby learn about her body. As she matures into a toddler, you may massage less frequently, yet the time you do spend massaging her will be cherished by your child and yourself. These quiet, intimate times will be an important part of the foundation from which will emerge a loving child, a loving teen, and eventually a loving adult. My sons, now in their 20s, still like me to give them a foot or neck massage, as they remember the love and connectiveness of touch to this day.

MY SON MARC AND DAUGHTER-IN-LAW, ALISA, HAVE BEEN MAS-SAGING my granddaughter since she was a few weeks old. On one of my trips to Michigan, I was going to baby-sit Shelby, then 18 months old, and Alisa told me, "Mom, Shelby didn't sleep last night. I think she may be coming down with something. Just feed her a bottle, let her watch her *Sesame Street* video, and then try to put her down for a nap."

I did as I was told, but Shelby just moped and squirmed. I held her, looked her in the eyes, and asked, "Shelby, would you like Grammy to give you a massage?" Well, quick as a wink she pulled off her socks, pulled up her shirt, and pointed to the cupboard where they kept the oil. I took the hint, warmed the oil, and proceeded to massage her feet and legs and then progressed up her body with slow strokes. To ask for more oil, she would point to the oil and make a noise ("Ugh-ugh"). It was winter in Michigan, so her skin was a little dry and absorbed the oil quickly. The massage went on for approximately 20 minutes, until all of a sudden she jumped off the sofa with a bundle of newfound energy and went off to play. I had to chase her to get her clothes back on! That experience showed me firsthand how healing loving touch can be. When I stimulated the hormones beneath her skin, she started to feel just fine.

On a more recent visit to Michigan, Shelby (now two years old) and I were playing with her dolls. She had a tiny jar of cream, which she opened and proceeded to gently smooth over her doll, giving her a mini-massage. When she was finished, she put her doll to bed, covered her up with a blanket, and said very sweetly, "Go sleepy now." Then, Shelby asked me to lie down—and before I knew what was happening, she removed my socks and started to massage my feet.

I was surprised by how much she was interested in massage. My son Marc confirmed my observation, and told me that Shelby insists on a back massage every night before going to bed—it really calms her down and gets her in the mood for sleep. Marc considers massage a blessing because it can be very difficult to settle an active child down for the night.

I marvel at how important massage has become for Shelby. Not only does she enjoy it for herself, but she wants to share it with her dolls and her family. It was very sweet for her to share it with me.

THE BENEFITS OF MASSAGE ARE NATURAL AND PROFOUND at the same time. As love is exchanged during the massage, the bond between two people becomes stronger and stronger. Fathers also find massage time a wonderful way to really connect to their baby. It gives them the opportunity to become more relaxed with their baby.

As previously stated, babies sleep better after a massage, and their immune systems strengthen with touch. Parents also benefit emotionally when they're able to increase their nurturing abilities and communication skills. As the providers of a child's basic needs, they want to learn to please their baby in a loving way. In turn, their children will develop a friendly and gentle manner that can help them mature into loving, caring adults.

Gail Perry, the businesswoman who resettled her business to her home, shares her experience of massaging her babies:

My husband and I always believed in massage for ourselves. Now we also do baby massage on our kids. When I was pregnant with my first child, my masseuse gave me an article showing different techniques for baby massage. So when I had my baby, I started to use those techniques to calm him. He loved it—it was so relaxing for him. Now he's almost three, and when he sees the masseuse come over to give my husband and me massages, he tries to get up on the table, too. And he likes to massage both me and his daddy.

When I massage my new baby girl, it's such a joy to see the bliss on her face. Both my kids are very active, but when I lay her down and start a massage, she just lies so still that I can tell she's transported. For me it's a way of connecting with my children; it's a time when I'm totally focused on them—there's nothing distracting me. To know that I'm doing something so soothing for those little rascals is great! Rubbing their tiny little feet and toes . . . you know, it's so wonderful to spend this time with them.

The importance of touch is obvious, especially with all the research that's being done. I just read an article on language and touch. It seems that babies who are rarely touched actually have smaller brains.

Their nerve connections are underdeveloped because nerve endings require stimulation in order to develop. The more babies are touched, the more brain cells and nerves are developed and connected—and it's all because of this physical attention. My kids are given loving touch all the time.

The more our children become accustomed to accepting massage and to the responses that touch can evoke, the more "in touch" they'll be with their own feelings. Grooming our children through touch to be aware of their internal reactions to external stimuli will enable them to make better health choices. Feelings can be a "health barometer," and assist in preventive health care. As our babies grow up with this awareness, the bond between mind and body will stay strong. It's our job to cultivate self-awareness in our children, because awareness is vital to maintaining bliss.

Shakespeare once wrote, "To thine own self be true." What better way is there to learn who we are but from the sensations of touch? Through massage, we can expand our self-awareness and become more sensitive to our feelings and thoughts. Teaching your baby to know herself begins with massage. What better time than the beginning to teach our children to listen to the messages their bodies send?

Summary

+ The caring touch of massage nurtures both mother and child.

+ Massage for pregnant women can relieve stress.

+ Pregnancy massage increases circulation, thus reducing swelling.

+ It reduces muscle tension in the neck and back while soothing the pregnant mother.

+ The embryo benefits from massage to the mother.

+ Your baby's first massage is actually the natural caress from movement in the womb.

+ The harmony felt in the womb can be re-established after birth through massage.

+ Loving touch assists motor and neural development.

+ Massaging your baby can help to relieve gastrointestinal disturbances as well as symptoms of colic.

+ Baby massage enhances the bond between parent and baby.

+++   +++

+ + + + + + + +

CHAPTER 5

+ + + + + + + +

Conscious Breathing and Yoga:
Infant Pre-Yoga Exercises and Yoga for Pregnancy

"Breath is the physical counterpart of the mind."

— Harish Johari

THE FIFTH SECRET IS CONSCIOUS BREATHING AND YOGA. Breathing can be more than just one of the basic bodily functions, involuntary and unconscious. By practicing conscious breathing, you stand to gain a greater awareness of yourself and others in the present moment. Breath acts as an accelerator of our body machinery—it's the motivator. Deep breathing causes blood to flow to all parts of the body, increasing mental alertness, enthusiasm, and physical vitality. It also benefits the nervous system, synchronizes bodily rhythms, relieves stress, and aids in spiritual realization. East Indian practitioners of yoga call deep breathing *prana,* and consider it the most powerful and fundamental element for personal change.

The word *yoga* means "union," the uniting of mind and body. Yoga is the combination of pranayama (breath techniques) and *asanas* (body postures). It helps us connect with our inner fountain of energy and promotes joy and well-being. One excellent guide to the practice, *Living and Yoga*, by Georg Feurstein and Stephan Bodian, explains: "Yoga is first and foremost the discipline of conscious living. When we take charge of our lives, we also tap into our inner potential for happiness, or what in Sanskrit is called *ananda*. This primal joy, which transcends the ego or personality, wells up in our hearts and infuses our entire being with vibrant energy—*life*."[1]

Effects of Conscious Breathing

If breathing is a natural phenomenon, why make a big deal about it? That was my question before I discovered all the different ways to breathe and their unique effects on the body—pregnant or not. Just as we've learned to be aware of how and what we eat so that our bodies are well nourished, we must be conscious of how we breathe to ensure our body's vital sustenance. Deep breathing helps our lungs expand, increasing their capacity to move oxygen, as well as life force, throughout our body. It regulates complex systems and organs—and even exercises our heart. Conscious inhaling and exhaling can quickly induce a relaxation response, resulting in the enhancement of immunity. Mindful breath can also coordinate our senses, renew our energy, and remind us of the inseparability of your mind and body.

The human body is a wondrous thing. When you begin to pay attention to your breath and the way it influences your body, you'll better understand what's going on inside *you*. You'll learn to tackle stress by taking a few deep, controlled breaths to rid yourself of the building tension in your shoulders and neck.

To further illustrate the importance of breathing, consider this: You may drink a few quarts of water and eat a couple pounds of food each day, but you breathe roughly 23,000 times in 24 hours, taking in about 4,500 gallons of air—much more if you exercise. Is it any wonder that the way you breathe can profoundly influence the health of your body and mind?

Barbara Manley Wheeler says that conscious breathing is a wonderful way for an expectant mother to quiet her mind and body. "The practice of pranayama deepens the mother's ability to relax, increases the capacity of her lungs, and prepares her for Lamaze breathing, which is wonderful training for labor."

Conscious breathing also strengthens the mother's bond with her unborn child. In the womb, the infant hears the vibrations of her mother's circulatory system and heartbeat. Naturally, the infant's bodily functions synchronize with the rhythm of her mother. They're united in this rhythm—and it's the breath that makes that beautiful connection possible.

IT'S GREAT TO PRACTICE SIMPLE CONSCIOUS-BREATHING TECHNIQUES wherever you are, no matter what you're doing—driving the kids around, negotiating a business deal, or standing in line in the grocery store. Simply focusing on breathing can reduce tension and anxiety and can even alleviate panic attacks. Best of all, you don't need a gym membership or an expensive class to learn to do the techniques.

However, you may find it valuable to designate a time and place for daily breath exercises. This way, you'll really make conscious breathing a part of your routine. Ideally, you'll want to practice pranayama twice a day for 20 minutes at a time, but don't feel guilty if you only have 10 minutes once a day—be assured that your body is appreciative.

Start the practice slowly and gradually; you may not be used to the extra oxygen you'll be taking in, and it could make you feel light-headed at first. Notice if you feel better with your eyes open or closed (some people may become dizzy when their eyes are shut). It's best not to do any kind of exercise with a full stomach—but if you must, eat lightly. There are no hard and fast rules, just be gentle with yourself and do what feels right. Your body will let you know what it needs.

UJJAYI BREATHING TECHNIQUE
(constriction of the throat)

Sit erect in a comfortable chair, feet flat on the ground. Your spine should be straight and your hands should rest apart on your lap. Close your eyes and focus on your breathing for a minute or two before starting.

Inhale deeply and slowly through your mouth, pulling the incoming air to the back of your throat. Slightly contract the back of your throat and hold your breath for a count of three. On the exhale, whisper the word *ha;* let the sound come from the back of your throat and let the *ha* last throughout the exhale. Now close your mouth and inhale only through your nose. On each exhalation, continue whispering *ha* from deep in your throat. Listen to your whispering breath as it helps you to expand and lengthen your lungs—it should sound smooth and light, like wind rushing through tall grass or a flock of birds passing close above your head. Do this for ten inhalations and ten exhalations. Sit quietly when you've completed this exercise. Are you calm? Exhilarated?

This technique brings with it a sense of control. As you become aware of the rhythm of your own breathing and of the sounds you make, you'll be more conscious of yourself and what you need to be balanced. If the sound of your breath is rough and raspy, that may be a warning of an impending cold or other illness. If the sound of your breath has a guttural, mucous sound, it could be the signal of an allergy or a Kapha imbalance.

NADI SHODHANAM BREATHING TECHNIQUE
(alternate nostril breath)

When you practice this technique, keep your spine straight and begin with a full inhalation through both nostrils. Close your right nostril with your right thumb and exhale through your left nostril. Then inhale through your left nostril and close it with the ring finger and the pinkie of your right hand. Remove your thumb and exhale through the right nostril. Next, inhale through the right nostril. Again, close the right nostril with the right thumb, release the left nostril, and exhale. Continue this process until you've completed ten inhalations and exhalations with each nostril.

You'll notice that one nostril always flows more freely than the other. This is natural. There's always an active nostril and a passive nostril, but left-right dominance changes throughout the day. The dominant, or active, nostril alternates every 90 to 120 minutes in a healthy individual.

Everyone experiences a subtle imbalance during this

alternation from time to time, but sometimes the imbalance is magnified and the nostril-alternating gets completely out of synch. This may be due in part to internal health factors (such as a cold or sinus congestion). According to a *Yoga International* magazine reprint published by the Himalayan Institute Press, "Each nostril has a different effect on the mind and body. The right nostril activates and warms; the left nostril has a receptive, cooling influence."[2] Therefore, in the practice of *Nadi Shodhanam,* the right nostril dominance is preferred for eating, conducting business, and working hard physically; while the left nostril dominance is best for listening, studying, resting, and healing.

This may sound strange, but nasal breathing affects your entire physiology. Left nostril and right nostril dominance correspond to the brain's right and left hemispheres, respectively. The cooling aspect of the left nostril stimulates the right hemisphere. The heating aspect of the right nostril stimulates the left hemisphere of the brain. In this way, body chemistry is influenced by the breathing capacity of each nostril. And if one of your nostrils is clogged and creates an imbalance in your breathing pattern, it may even have an effect on how you think.

Do your own experiments by noting which nostril is dominant during a given activity. How does food taste when your right nostril is dominant as opposed to when the left nostril is dominant? Apply this awareness to other activities, such as working, exercising, studying, and resting.

The heart and the nervous system are calmed by the practice of the alternate-nostril breath technique. Impurities are eliminated from the body through these exercises, just as cobwebs in a neglected flute are eliminated by blowing into the instrument. This breath exercise is a gentle way to get rid of anxiety and an easy way to calm your mind and body before going to sleep. I've used this technique in traffic jams and when I've been late for appointments. After I've alternated nostrils a few times, I've found that even the most stressful situations become manageable.

RESURRECTION BREATH TECHNIQUE

Turn your head to the left and push all the breath out of your stomach by forcefully breathing in deeply, then contracting your stomach in a rapid double exhalation (blowing out air in two successive exhalations). When you turn your head back to center, breathe naturally. Next, turn your head to the right and push all the breath out of your stomach, again in a rapid double exhalation. Return your head to the center position and breathe normally again.

Meditation begins more easily after this technique because it helps quiet the mind and releases tension in the body. By breaking the pattern of your normal breathing, this technique interrupts the habitual flow of emotions and thoughts. It helps you turn off the "noise" in your head—the constant thoughts, worries, emotions, and observations.

+++

"Yoga is without a doubt the master key
that unlocks the frontiers of the mind."

— B. K. S. Iyengar

Practicing Yoga

Practicing yoga during pregnancy is another way to connect with and focus on yourself and your baby. Yoga connects your soul with your baby's soul. Laura Yon is a yoga instructor in Cardiff-by-the-Sea, California, who taught yoga throughout her own pregnancy. When I interviewed her, she said:

> *When you're pregnant, doing yoga with specific postures is an incredible experience. Each time I did yoga, I noticed that my baby, Tara, was more active— it was as if she was doing it with me. It was so gentle and nice.*
>
> *Yoga opens up the pelvic area—softening the muscles and joints and bringing more oxygen and nutrients to that region. By concentrating on bringing energy and breath down to my abdomen, I felt really prepared for the birthing process.*

Wendy Gross, a yoga practitioner who owns and runs a yoga center in New Jersey, has worked with many pregnant women. Through the practice of yoga and pranayama, Wendy has seen pregnancy problems (such as migraines and insomnia) diminish, and new energy emerge:

> *Yoga balances the mind, body, and spirit. I've seen overweight women balance their weight, with the pounds gently falling away—and I've seen the reverse with underweight women. Yoga helps pregnant women build up the stamina and the suppleness they'll need in labor. Strength comes from the consistent practice of yoga and breath exercises.*

Several of the women I interviewed for this book expressed that yoga really helped them through pregnancy and delivery. My friend Denise McGregor told me: "I took a pregnancy yoga class because I'd heard that the squats and working with gravity could help facilitate giving birth. There's no question that yoga classes helped prepare my body."

Joy Star (the woman who healed herself after a miscarriage and went on to deliver a healthy baby) also insists that yoga is beneficial for expectant mothers:

> *I'd been doing yoga for many years before I got pregnant and I still consider myself drawn to it more than any other form of movement. During my pregnancy, my favorite position was the "dog," because it relieved the pressure on my back. I also loved the "squatting" pose, because it really stretches the inner thigh. Both of these exercises kept me limber and mentally prepared for labor and natural childbirth.*

WHEN PRACTICING YOGA, FIND A QUIET PLACE WHERE YOU'LL have room to stretch out. It's important that your environment is comfortable for squatting and kneeling, and roomy enough so that you can lie down and stretch out with ease. Set aside enough time and try not to rush through the asanas—you need to be present in the moment when you practice the positions. When you allow yourself time to unite your body and mind, then your movement becomes a meditation. If you focus on how you feel while doing the positions, you'll find the wisdom within them—and new energy and power will emerge.

If you're an energetic morning person like a Vata, you may prefer to do your yoga routine in the morning. If you're a slow-moving Kapha type, doing yoga and pranayama as soon as you wake up may energize you and strengthen your inner focus. Pittas may find that yoga and pranayama twice a day (in the morning for focus, and in the evenings for relaxation) works best. You be the judge. Learn to listen to your body.

Yoga Postures

There are many yoga positions that are especially beneficial during pregnancy; I've chosen the ones that I think have the greatest impact. (Please be aware that there are positions to avoid entirely.) According to yoga teacher Laura Yon, "Once you enter the second trimester, twisting should be eliminated because it can injure the sac, even rip it. Lying on your stomach isn't recommended for obvious reasons. Anything deep should be avoided, like deep back or forward bends."

Before starting any yoga program, ask your doctor if she thinks there are any stretching exercises you should avoid and any she recommends. Although she may not be familiar with yoga, she's familiar with you and your unique condition, so please listen to her counsel.

Yoga Preparation

+ Plan to practice the postures on an empty stomach.

+ Spend 15 to 20 minutes three times a week on the postures.

+ Remove your shoes and socks and wear loose, comfortable clothing (bare feet prevent slipping and roomy clothes allow free movement).

+ If practicing yoga outside, stay away from direct sun. Allow your body time to cool off before starting your yoga practice if you've been out in the sun.

SAMASTHITI

Samasthiti, or standing posture, is a good position to begin with. As you stand with arms at your sides, imagine a string of light going through your body, from the center of your head all the way down your spine. Close your eyes and feel the crown of your head pulled upward, as gravity anchors your tailbone to the center of the earth. Breathe in to that feeling seven times. Next, begin to

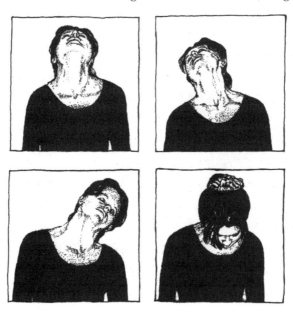

slowly roll your neck, gently revolving your head in a circle, still breathing in deeply and out slowly. Your breath should be natural and relaxed. This will release tension, free blocked energy, and break up calcium deposits. Balance is vital in yoga, so if you roll your neck seven times to the left, balance that with equal revolutions to the right.

FOLDING SQUAT

The folding squat is the next posture. It's recommended for strengthening the legs and opening the pelvic area for childbirth. Breathing in to this area also opens the chakras, which are said to be the life force or energy centers of the body.

Begin by standing with your feet parallel, hip-width apart. Inhale and exhale gently through your nostrils. Drop your head slowly forward, releasing your neck muscles. As you lower your head, let your spine fall downward, vertebra by vertebra. Inhale deeply now through the nostrils,

and exhale through your mouth, releasing all the air. With your hands and arms dangling loosely, bend your knees (to eliminate stress in the joints) and reach all the way to the floor. Your arms and feet will support you as you rest on all fours, allowing your uterus to suspend freely. Continue inhaling deeply and slowly, and bend your knees outward until you're squatting. Your legs should be open and your knees should be resting near your armpits. Feel the balance as your feet anchor you—feel the life flow. Place all your attention on your heartbeat, and breathe deeply. Your hands should be warm now because your blood and energy has flowed into them. Feel the blood flow into your tissues: Visualize the oxygen in your blood permeating and energizing your baby.

STANDING *KUNDALINI*

The third position is called the spirit posture, or the standing *Kundalini*. This is an important posture that can prepare you for conscious participation in birth, prevent tearing, and help you tone up after delivery.

Stand erect, with feet hip-width apart and arms relaxed at your sides. Inhale deeply, relaxing your vaginal muscles—on the exhalation, contract the vaginal muscles. Now inhale rapidly through your nose, as if you're sniffing. With each rapid sniff, progressively contract your thighs, the muscles of your buttocks, and your *pubococcygeal* muscle (the muscle that originates at your pubic bone and attaches at your *coccyx*, or tailbone). Then exhale and contract the vaginal muscles. As you focus on this area, you'll notice a sensation of total relaxation in your pelvis, abdomen, and thighs. You can practice this exercise anywhere and no one will know what you're doing. If you can manage to practice this exercise 100 times a day, you'll be doing much to prepare for an easier birth.

THIGH STRETCHES AND LUNGES

Yoga thigh stretches and lunges are excellent *asanas* during pregnancy because they give suppleness to the ligaments that help to push out the baby—preventing tearing and bruising during childbirth.

For the thigh stretch, stand with your legs straight, about hip-width apart. Now move your right leg two feet to the right and point your foot to the right. Inhale, and on the exhalation, bend your right knee. Feel the stretch along your right inner thigh. Inhale as you straighten the right knee.

Now alternate your legs so that your right leg is straight and your left leg is two feet to the left with your foot pointing left. Inhale, and on the exhalation bend your left knee. Repeat several times on each side. To increase the stretch, widen your stance.

Lunges take the thigh stretches a bit deeper. Stand straight with your legs together. Move your right leg forward about two to three feet, with your knee slightly bent. Keeping both feet flat on the floor, extend your arms forward. Use the back of a chair or the kitchen counter (or anything that's waist level) for balance. Inhale, and on the exhalation, bend your left leg until your knee touches the floor. If you can't reach the floor, that's okay—be gentle with yourself. Inhale through your nose, and at the same time, straighten your left leg to its original position. Repeat this lunge three times; switch legs.

THUNDERBOLT POSTURE

I'm particularly fond of doing the thunderbolt, or sit-on-heels posture, after lunging and stretching. This posture will help center you and combines meditation with the lunge posture.

After your last lunge, move so that you're kneeling on both knees, then bring your chest down to your knees. With your head resting on your knees, let yourself really feel the state your body is in. You may experience a bolt of energy pass through the top of your head down your spine.

Meditate or sit silently for a few minutes to balance yourself before getting up. Breathe in slowly and deeply a couple of times; close your eyes as you center yourself. Open your eyes slowly, and using the back of a chair to stabilize yourself, push upward until you're standing.

CAT STRETCH

The cat stretch is a good pelvic and spinal stretch. Start by getting on your hands and knees, with your back flat like a table. Proceed to gently arch your spine upward as you exhale. Relax on the inhalation, and then arch your back downward, with your head stretching up. Repeat these movements three times. This posture will help you keep a truly fluid spine during the intense bodily sensations and contractions you'll experience during labor.

THESE ARE JUST A FEW OF THE YOGA POSTURES THAT CAN provide tremendous benefits to you during the birthing process. However, it's important to remember that if yoga is new to you, your body may not be as supple as the bodies of practitioners who have performed the postures for many years. Go slowly and be gentle with yourself. Remember to check with your doctor before you start any new program. Again, beware of twisting, extreme arching, or inverting (that is, standing on your head) during this very precious time. Laura Yon cautions, "You shouldn't invert because you want to go with gravity in your pregnancy, delivery, and even when you have your menses. The natural flow is to go down and out. You're trying to help your baby get down, but when you invert, your energy is going in the opposite direction."

Listen to what your body tells you and be gentle with yourself. Intuitively you'll know when to stop. Yoga is most beneficial when done slowly, rhythmically, and with the breath as the primary leader.

The Feldenkrais Method®

The Mind/Body awareness that yoga promotes is very valuable. The Feldenkrais Method is another mind/body practice that's less well known, yet it's extremely beneficial to pregnant women.

✦✦✦

*"Our self image consists of four
components that are involved in every action:*

Movement
Sensation
Feeling
Thought

*When you affect one of them,
You affect all of them."*

— Moshe Feldenkrais

The Feldenkrais Method is a system of neuromuscular reeducation. In other words, it teaches your muscles and your nerves to alleviate pain and discomfort and increase mobility. The movements used are very slow and gentle because the body can learn how to move differently when there's less stress on the muscles. At the core of the method is Awareness Through Movement®—consisting of verbally directed exercises that bring about awareness and efficient body usage—the goal being for people to become conscious of their own muscles and skeletons.

During the later months of pregnancy, many women experience a heavy feeling, with backaches and a reduced capacity for breathing. As the months progress, these women start to wobble and move from side to side. Feldenkrais work can actually eliminate those difficulties by teaching people how to redistribute their weight.

Awareness Through Movement is verbally directed from a practitioner in a class or on a tape and consists of gentle exploratory movements in a sequence that's designed around a specific human function—such as bending, reaching, or walking. When you work one-on-one with a practitioner, she'll gently move your body while you stand or recline in a relaxed position. The practitioner will use subtle motions that teach your brain new ways to move, and you'll become aware of which muscles connect to certain bones. Through the gentle touch and movement of your skeleton, your nervous system is actually developing a new understanding of efficient movement.

The following is a Feldenkrais exercise that improves body awareness. You might want to use a tape player to record yourself reading the following directions—that way, you can play the tape back and focus on the movements and your body.

> *Lie on your back, stretch out your legs, and let your hands rest on the floor. Close your eyes and mentally scan your body. Notice what parts of your body are touching the floor: Do both shoulders touch the floor with the same weight? How does the right shoulder feel? The left shoulder? How is your back touching the floor? Does your lower back touch the floor at all? What area in your back doesn't touch the floor? Where does your right leg touch the floor? Where does your left leg touch the floor? Continue to scan your body without making any judgments.*
>
> *Now lie on your left side, bending your knees in front of your body at a right angle. Stretch both hands in front of your body, right on top of left. Now lengthen your right arm, reaching forward. Move your right arm forward and back. Where do you feel the movement? In your back? In your ribs? How do you feel along your right side, from your ribs down to your hip?*

Bring your right arm back, and without bending your elbow, let your right shoulder roll backward. Don't move your knees or hips. How do you feel? Is it easier to lengthen your arm or move it back?

Slowly turn on your back with legs outstretched and arms by your sides. Close your eyes and scan your body as you did at the beginning of the session. What parts of your back are touching the floor? Is there a difference from when you began?

Now change position so that you're lying on your right side. Bend your knees in front of your body at a right angle. Stretch both hands in front of you, left on top of right. Lengthen your left arm, reaching forward. Move your left arm forward and back. Feel the movement—where does it originate? In your back? In your ribs? How do you feel along your left side, from your ribs down to the hip?

Bring your left arm back without bending your elbow; let your left shoulder roll backward. Don't move your knees or hips. How do you feel? Is it easier to lengthen your arm or move it back?

Slowly turn on your back with legs outstretched and arms by your sides. Close your eyes and scan your body like you did at the beginning of the session. What parts of your back are touching the floor? Is there a difference from when you began?

Donna Ray Reese is a Feldenkrais practitioner who has given birth to two children. She told me:

The benefit [of Feldenkrais] to me when I was pregnant was that it brought about a change in posture so that I felt taller and more spacious. I could breathe and move with more ease. By the end of each lesson, I really didn't feel "pregnant." This continued up through the end of my term.

The body awareness that I had gave me a lot of control during the birthing experience. My husband is also a Feldenkrais practitioner, so during the moments when I'd bear down and push, he'd take hold of my head and gently organize my spine by repositioning my head. That way I'd be elongated, enabling my pushing to go directly to my pelvis where it was most effective.

When women give birth lying down, they tend to collapse and curve their backs. If they're sitting up, they tend to round their backs forward even more and bear down. Donna showed me how when you round your back, the pushing is actually directed to the lower back and not to the pelvis—so it's extremely inefficient in pushing your baby down in the direction that she needs to go. Instead, if you're able to elongate your spine, the force of the pushing actually goes down to the pelvis. You'll have an easier birth with a straight back.

Feldenkrais isn't necessarily a birthing practice, but the positioning of the spine in a straight line makes a great deal of sense. By following the principles of Feldenkrais, your spinal posture complements and eases the natural labor process. Donna explains:

In the Lamaze training, you take a deep breath and then bear down, releasing your breath—which in turn stops the pressure in your lungs and your ribs. It's my belief that if you do that, you can't bear down efficiently and push the baby down through the pelvis to the opening. If you hold your breath—even now as an experiment—you can feel the expansion of the rib cage, but you can't feel the bottom of your pelvis. So if you let the air out instead and you push your belly forward, the pressure goes down to the bottom of the pelvis.

Feldenkrais teaches a series of neck and jaw exercises that correspond with your perineum and your anus. By moving your mouth and jaw very softly, your perineum and your anus start to relax. Instead of the heightened tension created by blowing in and out, as in Lamaze, Feldenkrais helps to relax your mouth and subsequently relax your perineum area, which makes giving birth easier.

Tracy Ives, a certified athletic trainer and Feldenkrais practitioner, compares two of her children's births. The first was without Feldenkrais and the second was with Feldenkrais.

I'd pulled a groin muscle quite badly and tried everything to heal it. At the time I was working as an athletic trainer, and this problem really inhibited my practice. When I got pregnant, I was very uncomfortable. Then, someone told me about a Feldenkrais practitioner who was known to work wonders on tough cases. I tried to make an appointment with her, but she wouldn't work on me until I completed my pregnancy and recovered. It took me two years to regain my strength after that pregnancy and delivery. It wasn't a natural birth—they gave me drugs and I tore badly.

Finally, two years later, I started my Feldenkrais classes. I started having more function and resuming exercises I hadn't been able to do in years. I got pregnant with my second baby, and the pregnancy went smoothly. Despite my changing size and shape, I never felt awkward because my posture was balanced. My skeleton was working naturally, holding me up. I didn't have to rely on my muscles to do the work. I had a natural childbirth—no drugs, just endorphins.

Feldenkrais gave me a new life. I'm more physically and emotionally relaxed than ever. Subsequently, I've become a Feldenkrais practitioner, and I'm teaching my clients how they can have more bodily function with less muscular strain.

Throughout Europe, there are many Feldenkrais practitioners. In our country, the number of practitioners is growing. For more information about the Feldenkrais Method, write to: The Feldenkrais Guild, 524 Ellsworth St. SW, P.O. Box 489, Albany, OR 97321-0143.

Pre-Yoga for Baby

Once your baby is born and you've incorporated Touch Time (see Chapter 4) into your daily routine, there's one more thing you can do to prepare your baby for future healthy exercise: adding a pre-yoga stretch to the massage. After you've concluded the massage, you may want to try three pre-yoga exercises for your baby. They'll help her grow strong and maintain flexibility.

PRE-YOGA I

Remain in the baby massage position with your back against the tub, your infant facing you with her head on your knees. Hold on to your baby's hands, with her fist around your thumb and your fingers around her wrist to secure arms to side—at shoulder level. Be gentle and use no force.

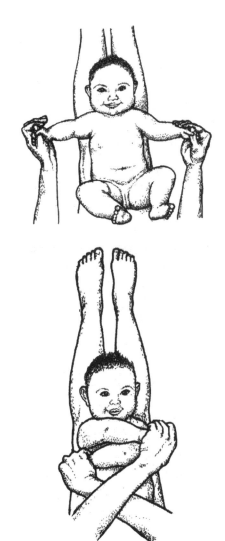

Now still holding your baby's hands, cross your hands and arms, left over right. In the process, your baby's arms will also cross right over left. Extend her baby's arms again, and then cross her left arm over right.

This is an excellent stretch for the arms, shoulders, and upper part of your baby's back.

Pre-Yoga II

Still sitting in the same position, hold your baby's left hand with your right hand, and her right foot with your

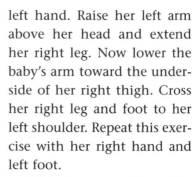

left hand. Raise her left arm above her head and extend her right leg. Now lower the baby's arm toward the underside of her right thigh. Cross her right leg and foot to her left shoulder. Repeat this exercise with her right hand and left foot.

This is an excellent hip and shoulder exercise. The leg and arm muscles, as well as shoulder and hip muscles, will release any tension from being in the womb or from crawling.

PRE-YOGA III

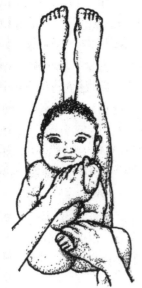

Hold your baby's right foot with your left hand and her left foot with your right hand. Bend her right knee, then bend her right foot over her left knee—or as high on her thigh as it will go with ease. Repeat with her left knee bending and crossing over to her right thigh. Return to the starting position, and now cross right foot over left, then left foot over right.

This exercise stretches the legs and hips and loosens the lower back.

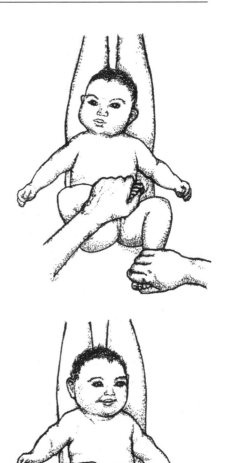

AS YOUR BABY GROWS INTO A TODDLER, SHE'LL BECOME MORE AWARE of things around her. She'll learn about different animals and the noises they make—as well as the differences in how they look. Parents, you now have the opportunity to teach your toddler the yoga postures with animal names translated from Sanskrit—you and your child can do them together. Make the session fun by talking about the animal and its posture. You can teach one at a time, and when you feel the time is right, teach another. Soon, you and your toddler will be playing guessing games as to which animal you're portraying.

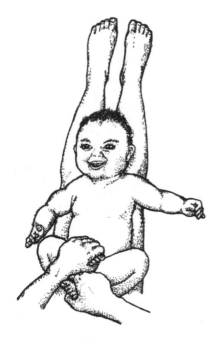

Here are the four simple animal postures: the fish pose, the hare pose (bunny), the dog pose, and the lion pose. The cat pose described earlier in this chapter can also be added to the animal postures you teach.

Fish Pose

Lie on your back. Place your palms on your thighs, resting your elbows on the floor beside you. Press on your elbows and lift your lower back off the floor. Lean your head back so that it touches the floor. Keep your chest lifted and arms relaxed. To come out of the pose, lift your head, lower your back, and relax.

Hare Pose

Kneel with your knees and feet together. Sit on your heels, and grasp your heels with your hands. Inhale deeply—as you exhale, bend forward. Place the top of your head on the floor, your forehead touching your knees (or as near your knees as possible), and keep your arms straight. Bring your upper torso as far forward as possible, concentrating on the spine between your shoulders. (You may want to touch the child's back when you explain the pose.) Inhale and return to the sitting position on your heels. Repeat and then relax.

DOG POSE

Start out on your hands and knees. Keeping your head down, push off on your arms—straightening your arms and legs at the same time. Your back should be as straight as possible as your body moves into an inverted V position. Return to all fours, go back to hare (bunny) pose and then stretch forward and relax.

LION POSE

Sit on your heels with your palms resting on your knees. Take a deep breath, then exhale—sticking out your tongue as far as it will go. Stiffen your fingers and spread them apart on your knees. Open your mouth and eyes wide, and tense your neck and throat and entire body. Hold for a few seconds, then relax.

+ + +

The above yoga postures are a wonderful way to play with your baby while teaching her a very valuable practice. On their own, these yoga postures are ways to develop flexibility and strength. But if you also talk about breathing into the tummy and make a game out of trying different breathing exercises, your toddler will have a head start on maintaining the union of body and mind.

Summary

+ Conscious breathing is another way to calm
  the mind.

+ Breath is called prana, or "life force," because it
  acts as an accelerator of our body machinery.

+ Pranayama is yoga breath. It's conscious breath.

+ Yoga means "union"—the union of the mind
  and the body.

+ Each nostril we breathe through has a different
  effect on the body: The right nostril warms and
  activates, the left nostril cools and is receptive.

+ Specific pregnancy yoga postures can aid in
  opening the abdomen by bringing more breath
  and nutrients to the pelvic area. This will help
  make the birthing process easier later on.

+ When pregnant, beware of (extreme) arching or
  inverting postures.

+ Doing yoga with your baby is a wonderful
  bonding experience.

+++   +++

+ + + + + + + +

CHAPTER 6

+ + + + + + + +

Nutrition:
Harmonizing Your Doshas

*"We are bound to our bodies
like an oyster to a shell."*

— Plato

THE SIXTH SECRET IS NUTRITION. Different people have different mind/body constitutions, and you must make sure that what you take in is best suited to your individual needs. Good nutrition means providing your body with what it requires to perform at a peak level. When you're pregnant, you're the spiritual/physical hostess of your baby; therefore, you must be consciously aware of the choices you make—not just for your own sake, but for the well-being and happiness of your child.

Ayurveda is based on the premise of balance. If your body is in perfect balance (chemically, structurally, emotionally, and spiritually), you'll be in perfect health. If you get out of balance because of food choices you've made, it's important to understand how to get back in balance before disease takes hold.

Good nutrition and proper digestion are fundamental

aspects of maintaining good health. Poor nutrition can result in indigestion—causing an imbalance. After all, your body's primary job is to reenergize and rebuild itself using the food you eat as fuel. If you suffer from indigestion, nutrients from food aren't reaching your tissues as they should.

Good digestion during pregnancy is of the utmost importance because it begets good health for you and your child. You should pay attention when choosing what to eat and how you eat it, and put into daily practice habits that are conducive to health—before, during, and after pregnancy.

✦✦✦

"Without proper diet, medicines are of no use.
With proper diet, medicines are of no need."

— Ayurvedic Proverb

Digestion and Disease: <u>Agni</u> and <u>Ama</u>

A strong and healthy digestive capacity in the body results from a steady *agni,* or digestive fire. A balanced agni ensures the absorption of nutrients from food and overall good health, while a disturbed agni is considered by Ayurveda to be one of the chief causes of disease. If your digestive fires are low, you may experience constipation, gas, gurgling, a feeling of "heaviness" after a meal, and loose stools. Digestive fires that are too high can inhibit the efficient breakdown of foods.

In contrast, you'll know your agni is balanced is if you feel good: Your complexion will glow and your eyes will shine; you'll have an ability to eat all foods; your urine will be clear (the color of lager); and your feces will be normal, without a strong smell.

Indigestion can create *ama,* the residue of physical and mental toxins. When digestion is poor, it leads to both the malabsorption of essential nutrients and the absorption of undigested or incompatible products. The resulting ama causes clogged channels, inferior tissues, and disturbed doshas—all of which will make you feel sick. In fact, ama is considered by the Ayurvedic health system to be the root of all disease because it disturbs and imbalances one or more doshas. Proper digestion, the result of a healthy agni, produces no buildup of ama. Early signs of ama are: dull skin, eyes that don't shine, teeth indentations on the side of the tongue, a bad taste in the mouth, strong bad breath, achy joints, chronic constipation, diarrhea, and loss of appetite. Have you ever seen a white coating on your tongue? That's ama. If the white coating is all over the tongue, the ama is throughout the body; if it's only on the back third of the tongue, then the colon has ama (a brownish-colored coating indicates a Vata disturbance).

To improve impaired agni, the following herbs and spices are recommended: black pepper, cardamom, cayenne, cinnamon, clove, horseradish, and mustard. Be careful to use these sparingly when you're pregnant and if you're a Pitta type, as they have a tendency to increase Pitta dosha—causing too much heat and fire in the digestive tract.

Ginger, both fresh and powdered, is an excellent spice to increase the power of digestion. (A word of caution: When pregnant and spotting, don't use. If you're having *any* trouble with your pregnancy, seek a doctor's advice.

An Ayurvedic physician will be able to read your pulse and know if ginger is right for you.) To make a wonderful balancing tea, boil a pinch of ginger in water over a low flame. Drink it before meals to whet your appetite or after meals to aid in digestion.

To reduce ama, use valerian to cleanse the colon and blood, winter cherry *(Withania somnifera)* to restore energy, and ginger (sparingly). There are other herbs recommended to improve ama, but they're too strong to use when pregnant.

To ensure proper digestion and keep your agni strong, you should eat what your body needs to stay balanced (we'll talk about this later in the chapter) and observe the following principles:

AYURVEDA'S SEVEN FOOD PRINCIPLES

1. Avoid cooking with honey. Although honey at room temperature is perfectly fine, heating it causes it to take on a gluelike consistency that's hard to digest. (You may sweeten tea with honey, just don't bake with it.)

2. Avoid ice-cold food and beverages since they impede, and interfere with, digestion.

3. Avoid eating or drinking dairy products after sunset because digestion becomes more difficult at that time of day.

4. Avoid leftovers; favor fresh food of the best possible quality.

5. Avoid discontented cooks—food should be prepared

by happy people and eaten in the most pleasant environment to ensure the best influence on your body's health.

6. Avoid cool, uncooked food; instead, choose warm, well-cooked foods.

7. Avoid foods that don't please the senses. Food should taste, smell, and look pleasing, delicious, appetizing, and desirable in order to inspire the best enzymes to digest your food.

It's important not to eat when you're angry or depressed. Emotional instability has a negative effect on the digestive system, which in turn prevents proper nutrition. Maintaining emotional stability is especially important when you're pregnant because your baby will interpret the world through your body. If your digestion is off because of emotional problems, your baby will be negatively affected.

Many of us rush through meals—we don't take the time to sit and enjoy the food we're consuming. This is disrespectful to the body because food doesn't digest properly when you're rushing; acidic enzymes can interrupt the natural digestive juices and cause malabsorption. The best way to eat is by sitting alone or with people you trust and find congenial. The more pleasant your environment, the better your digestion and health will be; therefore, music and fresh flowers—ambiance—add to your body's ability to absorb nutrients. Dr. Robert E. Svoboda, in his book *Prakruti: Your Ayurvedic Constitution,* writes: "A small amount of food presented to you lovingly will satisfy your soul, whereas large heaps of food from a fast-food restaurant may temporarily fill your belly but will leave your mind and spirit unsatisfied."[1]

The consciousness of the cook is very important, because a person who doesn't enjoy cooking isn't adding the ingredient of love to the recipe. Many restaurants serve food in such a hurried fashion that it's obvious that little care and thought have gone into its preparation. Our bodies appear to be affected not only by physical matter but also by the atmosphere around our bodies—things we can't see have a strong effect upon us. Knowing this, we can try to make better choices about not only what we eat, but *how* we eat.

Different flavors also influence the digestive process. According to Ayurveda, there are six tastes, and the digestive tract requires all six in order to function with maximum efficiency. The six tastes are: *sweet, salty, sour, pungent, bitter,* and *astringent*—and they're digested in this order. Thus, for optimal digestion, different flavors should be consumed at different parts of the meal and/or digestive process. A general rule is that heating tastes—salty, sour, and pungent—will aid in digestion by stimulating agni; the cooling tastes—sweet, bitter, and astringent—slow down the digestive process. (One exception to this rule is honey, which despite its sweetness is heating.)

The Three Stages of Digestion

According to Ayurveda, there are three stages of digestion, and by understanding them, you can help yourself absorb important nutrients more efficiently. The qualities of Vata, Pitta, and Kapha each influence a part of the digestive process—the Kapha stage is the first, the Pitta stage is second, and the Vata stage is third. (Keep in mind that this has nothing to do with your personal dosha—all people process food in the same order regardless of their mind/body type.)

The first stage of digestion, the taste stage, is in the mouth. This is the Kapha stage because the quality of Kapha (water) is found in the mouth and stomach. When you put something in your mouth, your taste buds get stimulated. Amazingly, the messages sent by those taste buds to the brain actually determine what kind of digestive juices your body secretes. Saliva helps to break down the food particles as the teeth pulverize the morsels.

Sweet is the first taste to be digested. Sugar in particular metabolizes faster than other tastes; therefore, it gets into the blood system immediately. That's why a person experiencing a low blood sugar attack, or *hypoglycemia,* is told to eat or drink something with a high sugar content (like orange juice). Ayurveda suggests that sweet foods (which, as the table found later in this chapter shows, include more than "sweets") should be eaten first. Sometimes when eaten after other foods, sweets stop the digestive process, allowing an undigested food mass to form and ferment; thus, the practice of having dessert directly at the end of a meal isn't recommended. It's better to wait 20 minutes or so before having dessert in order to allow the other foods a head start in digesting. In addition, if a slower-digesting food is eaten immediately before something sweet, flatulence may occur. Ideally, we should eat sweet foods first, allow them to digest, and then continue with our meal.

During the second stage of digestion, enzymes and hydrochloric acids associated with the stomach and small intestine process the food. This is the Pitta (fire) stage— also referred to as the "energetic" stage. Hydrochloric acid is capable of burning—beginning the "fire" of digestion, or agni stage. So it's important to have some some salty, sour, or pungent spices (heating tastes) in the middle of a meal because they increase the digestive power. Chutney and yogurt are good midmeal choices.

The third and last stage of digestion is the post-digestive stage. This is the Vata (air) stage, and it's when the long-term effects on the body are initiated. The nutrients are assimilated and used to break down the old body tissues and build up new ones.

Astringent and bitter tastes are digested last; because they're cooling tastes, they serve to put out the digestive fires (agni), close off the digestive process, and help produce stool. Black teas (or astringent herbal teas such as alfalfa, raspberry leaf, or strawberry leaf) are good for this purpose.

Eating According to the Doshas

Because of all the changes that are taking place in our bodies during pregnancy, it's especially important to keep balanced during those nine months. For instance, if you have a strong Pitta body-type, modify and calm your fiery attributes through foods that are cooler and will pacify Pitta. Your baby's digestive system can be negatively affected if your own body becomes imbalanced. Just as a mother's thoughts and emotions can have either nurturing or damaging effects on her baby, so can food. That's why we must understand how the various qualities of our foods (including taste) affect our bodies.

Vata

A Vata-balancing diet is considered the best way to eat during pregnancy. Even if you aren't Vata dominant, it's best to keep your body moist, warm, and calm when you're expecting—your womb requires extra moisture and warmth. It's in this type of environment that the fetus will thrive. Fresh fruits and vegetables are recommended, but they should be cooked and enjoyed warm. Clarified butter *(ghee)* and warm milk are highly recommended during pregnancy; as are sweet tastes such as breads, grains, rice, and sweet fruits. Honey and raw sugar are preferred. Refined sugar should be avoided, as should spicy or hot foods and raw, leafy vegetables.

A Vata-dominant constitution has a tendency toward dryness, chilliness, and erratic eating patterns. When Vata increases, it gets out of balance. Enjoy meals that are warm, foods that are well cooked, and regimes that bring regularity to the body's system. The quality of dryness in dried fruits and in some fresh fruits (such as cranberries, raw apples, pears, persimmons, and pomegranates) increases Vata and should be avoided. Also avoid unripe fruits and dried beans and lentils. Fruits that are good for Vata types are: cooked apples and applesauce, apricots, avocados, bananas, berries, cherries, pineapple, and plums. These fruits have a moisturizing quality.

Frozen, raw, and dried vegetables, as well as artichokes and beet greens, aren't good for Vata types or mothers-to-be. Cooked vegetables good for Vata types and pregnant women are: asparagus, beets, carrots, celery, cilantro, garlic, green beans, okra, onions, radishes, turnips, sweet potatoes, cooked spinach, squash, and cooked tomatoes—to name a few.

Most dairy food is good because it counteracts the Vata tendency toward dryness. Especially good dairy products are: butter, buttermilk, soft cheese, cottage cheese, ghee, goat cheese, ice cream, and yogurt (only if diluted and spiced).

Pitta

When pregnant, it's especially important to keep in balance Pitta's tendency to get hot. Too much heat—the kind generated through excess hot, spicy foods—can make a pregnancy unstable and lead to miscarriage. Pittas should avoid humidity and try to stay cool. They should avoid hot spices, alcohol, and fried foods. Fresh fruits and vegetables should be emphasized, along with whole grains and ample amounts of milk and milk products. Dairy foods are usually cooling in nature, and an occasional ice cream is often a favorite for Pitta types. Astringent, bitter, and sweet tastes should be used in food choices. Fresh air is an important ingredient in balancing a Pitta dosha because it cools you off. If you're a Pitta and are pregnant, the suggestions for Vata should be used moderately. Warm foods are okay, but avoid hot foods. Adhere to regular eating and sleeping habits, and do everything in moderation.

Kapha

The Kapha dosha doesn't need to be addressed during pregnancy unless it appears to be out of balance by extreme lethargy, excessive mucus, and allergy symptoms. Many attributes of the Kapha constitution are naturally synonymous with the requirements of pregnancy, as Kaphas are blessed with stamina, strength, and a calm nature. They're slower, and when pregnant it's important to slow down; they have a need for more sleep than the other doshas, and that's desirable because rest nurtures the growing baby.

During pregnancy it's not advisable to stimulate Kapha through dietary adjustments. If lethargy persists to a fault, frequent shifts in schedules and activities can help eliminate the propensity to get stuck in a rut—emotionally or physically.

TO AID YOU IN MAKING FOOD CHOICES, ON THE FOLLOWING PAGES you'll find a list of foods, including their taste, quality, and whether or not they're recommended for each dosha. Keep in mind that the headings Vata, Pitta, and Kapha refer to people with a predominant dosha. If a food is labeled "eat sparingly" for your dosha, that means to limit this food in your diet. If your dosha is recommended to eat a food moderately, this means you can enjoy this specific item, but no more than three times a week. If a food is labeled "eat freely" for your dosha, then there's no limit to the quantity you may consume. Remember that you should include all six tastes in each meal, and ideally consume them at specific points during the meal.

TASTES OF MEAT AND FISH

	VATA	PITTA	KAPHA
Animal oils/ lard (sweet)	eat moderately	eat moderately	eat sparingly

TASTES OF MEAT AND FISH *(cont'd.)*

	VATA	PITTA	KAPHA
Beef (sweet)	eat moderately	eat sparingly	eat sparingly
Chicken (sweet)	eat moderately	eat moderately	eat sparingly
Duck (sweet)	eat freely	eat sparingly	eat sparingly
Eggs (sweet)	eat freely	eat sparingly	eat sparingly
Fish (sweet/salty)	eat freely	eat moderately	eat sparingly
Lamb (sweet)	eat moderately	eat sparingly	eat sparingly
Pork (sweet)	eat sparingly	eat sparingly	eat sparingly
Shellfish (sweet)	eat freely	eat sparingly	eat sparingly
Turkey (sweet)	eat moderately	eat moderately	eat moderately

TASTES OF VEGETABLES

	Vata	Pitta	Kapha
Artichokes (sweet/ astringent)	eat moderately	eat freely	eat moderately
Asparagus (sweet/bitter/ moderately astringent)	eat moderately	eat freely	eat freely
Beans, green (sweet/ astringent)	eat sparingly	eat freely	eat freely
Beets (bitter/sweet)	eat freely	eat moderately	eat freely
Broccoli (bitter/ astringent)	eat sparingly	eat freely	eat freely
Carrots (sweet/ pungent)	eat freely	eat moderately	eat freely
Corn (sweet)	eat sparingly	eat moderately	eat moderately
Eggplant (bitter)	eat moderately	eat moderately	eat moderately

TASTES OF VEGETABLES *(cont'd.)*

	VATA	PITTA	KAPHA
Lettuce (bitter/ astringent)	eat sparingly	eat freely	eat freely
Mushrooms (sweet/ astringent)	eat sparingly	eat freely	eat freely
Onions (sweet/ pungent)	eat moderately	eat moderately	eat freely
Peas (sweet/ astringent)	eat sparingly	eat freely	eat freely
Potatoes (astringent)	eat sparingly	eat moderately	eat moderately
Spinach (bitter)	eat moderately	eat moderately	eat moderately
Squash (sweet)	eat sparingly	eat moderately	eat moderately
Tomatoes (sweet/sour)	eat sparingly	eat moderately	eat moderately
Zucchini (sweet)	eat sparingly	eat freely	eat sparingly

TASTES OF FRUITS

	Vata	Pitta	Kapha
Apples (sweet/ astringent)	eat moderately	eat freely	eat freely
Apricots (sweet/sour)	eat moderately	eat sparingly	eat sparingly
Bananas (sweet/ astringent)	eat moderately	eat sparingly	eat sparingly
Berries:			
Blueberries (sweet/ astringent)	eat freely	eat freely	eat sparingly
Cherries (sweet/sour)	eat freely	eat sparingly	eat sparingly
Cranberries (astringent/ sweet)	eat sparingly	eat freely	eat freely
Raspberries (sweet/sour)	eat freely	eat moderately	eat sparingly
Strawberries (sweet/sour/ astringent)	eat freely	eat freely	eat sparingly

TASTES OF FRUITS *(cont'd.)*

	VATA	PITTA	KAPHA
Figs (sweet/ astringent)	eat freely	eat freely	eat sparingly
Grapefruit (sour)	eat freely	eat moderately	eat freely
Lemons (astringent/ sour)	eat freely	eat sparingly	eat sparingly
Melons (sweet)	eat sparingly	eat freely	eat sparingly
Nectarines (sweet/sour)	eat freely	eat moderately	eat sparingly
Peaches (sweet/sour)	eat moderately	eat sparingly	eat sparingly
Pears (sweet)	eat moderately	eat freely	eat moderately
Plums (sweet/sour)	eat moderately	eat moderately	eat sparingly
Raisins (sweet)	eat sparingly	eat moderately	eat freely

TASTES OF DAIRY

	Vata	Pitta	Kapha
Butter (sweet)	eat freely	eat freely	eat sparingly
Buttermilk (sour/ astringent)	eat freely	eat sparingly	eat moderately
Cheese (sweet)	eat moderately	eat moderately	eat sparingly
Cottage cheese (sweet)	eat freely	eat freely	eat sparingly
Cream (sweet)	eat freely	eat freely	eat sparingly
Ghee (sweet)	eat freely	eat freely	eat moderately
Ice cream (sweet)	eat sparingly	eat sparingly	eat sparingly
Milk (sweet)	eat freely	eat moderately	eat moderately
Sour cream (sweet/sour)	eat freely	eat sparingly	eat sparingly
Yogurt (sour)	eat freely	eat sparingly	eat sparingly

TASTE OF GRAINS

	Vata	Pitta	Kapha
Barley (sweet)	eat moderately	eat freely	eat freely
Buckwheat (sweet)	eat moderately	eat moderately	eat moderately
Corn (sweet)	eat moderately	eat moderately	eat moderately
Couscous (sweet/ astringent)	eat sparingly	eat freely	eat sparingly
Flour, white (sweet/ astringent)	eat sparingly	eat sparingly	eat sparingly
Flour, whole wheat (sweet/ astringent)	eat freely	eat freely	eat sparingly
Granola (sweet/ astringent)	eat sparingly	eat moderately	eat freely
Millet (sweet/ astringent)	eat moderately	eat moderately	eat moderately
Oats (sweet)	eat freely	eat freely	eat sparingly

TASTE OF GRAINS *(cont'd.)*

	VATA	PITTA	KAPHA
Rice (sweet)	eat freely	eat moderately	eat sparingly
Rye (sweet/ astringent)	eat sparingly	eat moderately	eat moderately

TASTES OF BEANS AND LEGUMES

	VATA	PITTA	KAPHA
Aduki beans (sweet/ astringent)	eat moderately	eat freely	eat freely
Chickpeas (sweet/ astringent)	eat moderately	eat moderately	eat sparingly
Fava beans (sweet/ astringent)	eat sparingly	eat freely	eat freely
Kidney beans (sweet/ astringent)	eat moderately	eat moderately	eat moderately
Lentils (sweet/ astringent)	eat sparingly	eat sparingly	eat freely

TASTES OF BEANS AND LEGUMES *(cont'd.)*

	VATA	PITTA	KAPHA
Lima beans (sweet/ astringent)	eat moderately	eat freely	eat freely
Mung beans (sweet/ astringent)	eat freely	eat freely	eat moderately
Peanuts (sweet/ astringent)	eat sparingly	eat sparingly	eat moderately
Pinto beans (sweet/ astringent)	eat sparingly	eat moderately	eat moderately
Soy beans (sweet/ astringent)	eat sparingly	eat moderately	eat freely
Split peas (sweet/ astringent)	eat sparingly	eat moderately	eat moderately
Tofu (sweet/ astringent)	eat moderately	eat freely	eat moderately

TASTES OF CONDIMENTS

	VATA	PITTA	KAPHA
Carob (sweet/ astringent)	eat moderately	eat sparingly	eat sparingly
Chocolate (pungent/ bitter)	eat moderately	eat freely	eat freely
Cornstarch (sweet)	eat moderately	eat sparingly	eat sparingly
Ketchup (sweet/sour)	eat moderately	eat moderately	eat moderately
Mayonnaise (sour/sweet)	eat moderately	eat moderately	eat moderately
Mustard (pungent)	eat freely	eat sparingly	eat freely
Salt (salty)	eat moderately	eat sparingly	eat sparingly
Vegit (Seasoning) (all tastes)	eat moderately	eat moderately	eat moderately
Vinegar (sour)	eat moderately	eat sparingly	eat sparingly

TASTES OF OILS

	Vata	Pitta	Kapha
Almond (sweet/bitter)	eat freely	eat sparingly	eat sparingly
Avocado (sweet/ astringent)	eat freely	eat moderately	eat sparingly
Canola (sweet)	eat sparingly	eat moderately	eat freely
Coconut (sweet)	eat sparingly	eat moderately	eat moderately
Corn (sweet)	eat sparingly	eat moderately	eat moderately
Flaxseed (pungent/ sweet)	eat freely	eat sparingly	eat freely
Margarine (sweet)	eat sparingly	eat moderately	eat moderately
Olive (sweet)	eat freely	eat moderately	eat sparingly
Peanut (sweet)	eat moderately	eat sparingly	eat moderately
Safflower (sweet/ pungent)	eat freely	eat moderately	eat freely

TASTES OF OILS *(cont'd.)*

	VATA	PITTA	KAPHA
Sesame (sweet)	eat freely	eat sparingly	eat sparingly
Soy (sweet/ astringent)	eat moderately	eat moderately	eat moderately
Sunflower (sweet)	eat moderately	eat moderately	eat freely

TASTES OF HERBS AND SPICES

	VATA	PITTA	KAPHA
Allspice (pungent)	eat freely	eat sparingly	eat freely
Anise (pungent)	eat sparingly	eat sparingly	eat freely
Basil (pungent)	eat freely	eat moderately	eat freely
Bay leaf (pungent)	eat freely	eat sparingly	eat freely
Caraway (pungent)	eat freely	eat moderately	eat freely
Cayenne (pungent)	eat moderately	eat sparingly	eat freely

TASTES OF HERBS AND SPICES *(cont'd.)*

	Vata	Pitta	Kapha
Cinnamon (pungent/ bitter)	eat freely	eat moderately	eat freely
Cloves (pungent)	eat freely	eat moderately	eat freely
Coriander (pungent/ bitter)	eat freely	eat freely	eat freely
Cumin (pungent)	eat freely	eat moderately	eat freely
Dill (pungent)	eat moderately	eat moderately	eat moderately
Fennel (pungent)	eat freely	eat freely	eat moderately
Garlic (all but sour)	eat freely	eat sparingly	eat freely
Ginger (pungent/ sweet)	eat freely	eat sparingly	eat freely
Horseradish (pungent)	eat moderately	eat sparingly	eat freely
Lemongrass (pungent/sour)	eat moderately	eat moderately	eat moderately

TASTES OF HERBS AND SPICES *(cont'd.)*

	VATA	PITTA	KAPHA
Marjoram (pungent)	eat freely	eat sparingly	eat freely
Mint (pungent)	eat moderately	eat moderately	eat moderately
Mustard (pungent)	eat moderately	eat sparingly	eat freely
Nutmeg (pungent/ astringent)	eat freely	eat moderately	eat moderately
Oregano (pungent)	eat freely	eat sparingly	eat freely
Paprika (pungent)	eat moderately	eat moderately	eat moderately
Peppermint (pungent)	eat moderately	eat moderately	eat moderately
Poppyseed (pungent/ astringent/ sweet)	eat freely	eat sparingly	eat freely
Rosemary (pungent/ bitter)	eat freely	eat moderately	eat freely

TASTES OF HERBS AND SPICES *(cont'd.)*

	VATA	PITTA	KAPHA
Saffron (pungent)	eat moderately	eat moderately	eat freely
Sage (pungent)	eat freely	eat sparingly	eat freely
Tarragon (pungent)	eat freely	eat sparingly	eat freely
Tea, Chamomile (pungent/ bitter)	eat freely (during first 3 months of pregnancy and postpartum)	eat freely (during first 3 months of pregnancy and postpartum)	eat freely (during first 3 months of pregnancy and postpartum)
Turmeric (pungent/ bitter/ astringent)	eat moderately	eat moderately	eat freely

Note: Spices and herbs can add to your meal the extra taste you may require in order to have all six tastes within your meal. They're a wonderful way to add flavor and at the same time satisfy your six taste requirements for good health.

TASTES OF NUTS AND SEEDS

	VATA	PITTA	KAPHA
Almonds (sweet/bitter)	eat freely	eat sparingly	eat sparingly
Brazil nuts (sweet)	eat freely	eat sparingly	eat sparingly
Cashews (sweet)	eat freely	eat sparingly	eat sparingly
Coconut (sweet)	eat moderately	eat freely	eat moderately
Filberts (sweet)	eat freely	eat sparingly	eat sparingly
Macadamia nuts (sweet)	eat freely	eat freely	eat freely
Pecans (sweet/bitter)	eat freely	eat sparingly	eat sparingly
Pine nuts (sweet)	eat freely	eat moderately	eat sparingly
Pistachios (sweet)	eat freely	eat sparingly	eat sparingly
Sesame seeds (sweet)	eat freely	eat moderately	eat moderately
Sunflower seeds (sweet/bitter)	eat moderately	eat freely	eat moderately

TASTES OF NUTS AND SEEDS *(cont'd.)*

	Vata	Pitta	Kapha
Walnuts (sweet)	eat freely	eat sparingly	eat sparingly

Note: Nuts and seeds can be easily overeaten because they're so easy to prepare and so fun to snack on. They can affect your digestive tract if eaten indiscriminately. I suggest adding the right nut or seed to grains or a salad or vegetable as you would a garnish or seasoning.

TASTES OF BEVERAGES

	Vata	Pitta	Kapha
Alcohol (pungent/ bitter/ sour/sweet)	drink moderately	drink sparingly	drink sparingly
Coffee (pungent/ bitter)	drink sparingly	drink sparingly	drink moderately
Juice, citrus (sweet/sour)	drink freely	drink sparingly	drink sparingly
Juice, other fruit (sweet/ astringent)	drink sparingly	drink freely	drink freely

TASTES OF BEVERAGES *(cont'd.)*

	VATA	PITTA	KAPHA
Mineral water (bitter)	drink sparingly	drink freely	drink freely
Soft drinks (sweet)	drink sparingly	drink sparingly	drink sparingly
Tea, black (bitter/sweet/ astringent)	drink sparingly	drink freely	drink freely
Tea, herbal (spicy)	drink freely	drink sparingly	drink freely

THE QUALITIES OF THE TASTES ARE EXTREMELY IMPORTANT when planning a meal—they should match your dosha. But when selecting foods, you should also be mindful of the state your body is in. For example, if you have excessively oily skin and are having loose, moist, mucous bowels, you may be experiencing too much moisture in your body, associated with excess Kapha. In that case, it would be best to choose foods with dry qualities and tastes, such as pears, apricots, berries, millet, or barley.

If your body shows signs of dryness, such as dry skin and hair; brittle nails; or hard, dry stools, you probably have a Vata imbalance. Avoid drying foods and tastes, steam your vegetables to add moisture, and add oil or ghee to your food. Eating foods such as sesame seeds, nuts, rice, and milk will help decrease the dryness of Vata—thereby balancing that aspect.

Ghee, or clarified butter (butter without the milk solids) is used extensively in Ayurvedic cooking. Ghee adds moisture to the dry Vata and balances Pitta without increasing its fire. It can be kept at room temperature for an indefinite period; as long as you insert only a clean, dry utensil into it, the ghee won't mold. If a moist or wet utensil comes in contact with the ghee, it won't last. If you choose to refrigerate it, the ghee will turn very hard and a knife will be needed to extract the desired portion. Ghee is very healthful when eaten in moderation.

GHEE

Ghee can be used as a cooking oil, as flavoring in place of butter, and as a digestive stimulator in small quantities. To make ghee, melt one pound of unsalted butter over low heat. Raise the heat to medium after the butter has completely melted. When foam rises, skim it off the top, then lower heat for about ten minutes. When moisture and milk solids are cooked out of the butter, it's ready to be used.

These guidelines may seem a bit confusing at first, but with a little practice you'll be able to eat for maximum nutrition in no time. And once you reap the benefits of eating this way, you'll agree that it's worth the effort. Once I got the hang of this simple yet practical way of handling nutrition, my personal health improved. Alisa, my daughter-in-law, was amazed at how easy it was to plan balanced meals with these principles of tastes, qualities, elements, and doshas. The main thing to remember is that everything is relative to your individual digestive strengths. Pay attention to your body, because self-observation is the best teacher.

Listening to your body with the knowledge of mind/body types will ensure a healthier life for you and your baby. In many cases, the human body is smarter than we give it credit for—especially when it comes to knowing what it needs. For example, the hormonal changes that occur at the beginning of pregnancy emulate Vata, the ideal conditions for creating a new life. Later in pregnancy, Kapha-like changes take place in the body to prepare for breast-feeding (the state of calm is what breast-feeding is all about). So listen to your cravings—they can be the key to balancing your doshas. Honor all cravings, but do so in moderation. According to Ayurveda, during pregnancy your cravings are actually your baby's desires; by responding to your cravings, you may actually be giving your baby what she needs.

Nurturing Your Baby: Breast-Feeding

The American Academy of Pediatrics recommends breast milk as a near-perfect source of nutrition for the infant. And breast-feeding is very nurturing to your own body as well: It helps shrink your uterus back to its normal size and usually helps you lose the weight you gained during pregnancy. However, every mother must make her own decision whether to breast-feed or not. Researching the advantages and disadvantages will help you make a more educated decision.

If a mother has taken drugs or is HIV-positive, *breast-feeding is not recommended* because the drug or disease can be transmitted to the baby through the milk. Women with breast augmentation run a risk of leaking silicone through their breast milk and probably should not breast-feed. There's been some controversy on this issue, but to play it safe for the health of your child, I wouldn't recommend breast-feeding if you've had implants.

In our society, many new mothers go back to work shortly after the birth of their babies; subsequently, a formula diet and bottle-feeding seems their only choice. But there are alternatives to formula, such as pumping and storing your breast milk so that the caregiver can bottle-feed *your* milk to *your* baby. Many offices are accommodating new mothers with extended lunch hours as well as day-care facilities adjacent to the workplace for convenience. Whichever options are open to her, each mother should make an educated decision on how her baby will be fed. (*The Nursing Mother's Companion,* by Kathleen Huggins,[2] is a good source information for mothers who choose to breast-feed.)

Rebecca Cortez, a certified lactation educator, has this to say:

> *I tell the women I teach that the baby's brain is still growing when you're postpartum, and breast milk is the best food for the baby's brain. If you breast-feed for up to six months, the baby's immune system will build up with antibodies that fight off disease. If you breast-feed longer, then the antibodies will last longer.*
>
> *Although babies do grow on processed infant formulas, formula manufacturers are continually challenged to include all of the nutrients in breast milk that scientists are gradually identifying as important to infant growth and development. But artificial infant milks, whether based on cow's milk or soybeans,*

will never be able to duplicate nature's formula. Human milk contains proteins that promote brain development and specific immunities against human illness. In contrast, cow's milk contains proteins that favor muscular growth and specific immunities to bovine (cow) disease. Babies, like all young mammals, do best with milk from their own species.

Formula diets for babies increase their risk for ear infections, respiratory illnesses, and even diarrhea. Recently, scientists have found evidence that learning disorders are experienced more often by people who were fed an artificial formula diet as babies. On average, adults that were breast-fed as infants have a lower cholesterol level. Recommendations by the American Academy of Pediatrics state that *only* breast milk should be fed to the infant for the first four to six months of life and continued for the remainder of the first year when possible.

I breast-fed only one of my three children (my oldest son, Marc) and I had a wonderful experience sharing those times of closeness with him. Witnessing your baby grow from the milk produced by your body is a very special feeling. Although I had wanted to breast-feed my second son, Ryan, my doctors discouraged me because I had contracted diabetes. They told me that they wanted my body to return to normal so that they could treat my diabetes. I've found out in recent years that had I breast-fed Ryan, my body would have returned to normal faster. For some diabetic mothers, breast-feeding can decrease their need for insulin, balancing their bodies and resulting in a remission-like state.

When I asked Rebecca what other advantages there were to breast-feeding, she replied, "If you don't breast-feed, it's going to be harder to work off the fat that you've gained. Women develop extra fat pads on their back as well as other places—the body uses that fat and converts it to breast milk."

Thinking back on my two experiences, breast-feeding and bottle-feeding, I do remember getting back in shape faster after giving birth to Marc, the one I breast-fed. My third child, Angie, was adopted, and at that time the issue never came up. Today, however, it's understood that it's possible to stimulate the breasts to produce milk by allowing the baby to suck. In those situations, a supplement is needed to ensure proper nutrition.

Csilla Heiligenberg Crouch, a young businesswoman, has been nursing her 16-week-old son, Jenson, since birth, and she insists that it's a very easy way to nourish her baby. Explaining what she meant by "easy," she said:

> It's extremely convenient. I never have to worry about where the food is. I don't have to worry about bottles and mixing up formula, or taking something along with us if we go out. It's always readily available and at the right temperature. At night I just lift him out of his bassinet, feed him, and put him back to sleep. I don't even have to get out of bed unless I need to change him. He really enjoys it, and so do I.

Csilla admitted that the first couple of weeks of nursing were hard to adjust to because both she and Jenson were learning something new. She said it was challenging and she was sore, but her friends had assured her that the discomfort would subside after the first week. "I was warned that a lot of people give up during that first week, but I was determined not to give up." Her discomfort did subside after the first six days, and from then on she was blissfully committed.

At first, I was really concerned about where I would feed him in public—that it might be awkward. But I've gotten used to that. A couple of times I was in the grocery store when he got hungry, so I parked my basket, went out to my car, and sat in the backseat and fed him. Once he was content, I went back in the store and resumed my business. With a little practice, I became very discreet and more graceful. Today I think people are becoming more aware of how beneficial breast-feeding is, and they seem to respect you for going to the trouble of nursing.

Csilla is one of the new breed of professional women who works out of her home. She has a flexible schedule and manages to keep Jenson a priority. Other mothers who work away from their homes find that expressing their milk into bottles and refrigerating it enables them to both work and breast-feed. The evening or nighttime feeding is the most comforting for these mothers, because baby is at last settled in their arms—and nourished next to their heart.

There are many women who choose not to breast-feed, or can't due to medical reasons; if you're one of them, you know that your challenge requires more investigation into alternative methods of bonding with and nourishing your child. One important effort you can make is to hold your baby close to your breast when bottle-feeding. Many mothers find it easier to prop bottles up for their babies to feed themselves, but there's no way a nursing mother can prop up her breast and go off to do other chores. It's important when bottle-feeding to make sure that your contact with your baby is as close and personal as if you were nursing. The baby needs that attention. It's always been a pet peeve of mine to see babies walking around sucking on bottles, because eating time should be an opportunity for closeness and nurturing, not just pacifying a baby by giving her a bottle to walk around with. Nature's plan is the most harmonious way. If breast-feeding isn't possible for you, try to include some special bonding time in your day. Speak to your OB/GYN or pediatrician for ways to achieve intimacy between you and your baby, and research the variety of formulas on the market today.

WE ALL WANT THE BEST FOR OUR CHILDREN, AND I BELIEVE that the following affirmations can help us focus on the healthiest choices:

+ Let us choose what's best for our bodies rather what's faster to eat.

+ Let us respect our bodies and know whether the stress we feel is positive or negative.

+ Let us choose to listen to and love our bodies again.

+ Let us allow and encourage our children to stay in touch with the needs of their bodies and to love their bodies for communicating those needs.

+ Let us give our children choices instead of directives and know that most of the time they'll choose what's best for them.

Summary

+ Good nutrition refers to what we put into our bodies that best serves us.

+ Nutrients can't reach the tissues in a body that suffers from indigestion.

+ Ginger is an excellent spice to increase the power of digestion.

+ There are three stages of digestion: taste, energetic, and post-digestive. According to Ayurveda, there are six tastes that should be consumed during every meal to assist in digestion.

+ Even if you're not Vata dominant, a Vata-balancing diet is the best way to eat when pregnant because it will keep your body moist, warm, and calm.

+++ +++

✦ ✦ ✦ ✦ ✦ ✦ ✦ ✦

CHAPTER 7

✦ ✦ ✦ ✦ ✦ ✦ ✦ ✦

Nurturing Yourself and Your Newborn:
Labor, Birth, and the Postpartum Period

*"The oldest oracle in Greece, sacred to the
Great Mother of Earth, sea, and sky, was named
Delphi, from delphos, meaning 'womb.'"*

— Barbara Walker

THE SEVENTH SECRET IS NURTURANCE. It's important to nurture yourself throughout your maternal journey— through pregnancy, labor/delivery, and postpartum— because your baby is one with your bliss. By carefully selecting and participating in the practices laid out in this book, your baby will get a healthy start while growing inside your body. As you take time for your own well-being, massage yourself, and listen to your emotional and physical needs, the baby in your womb will receive the endorphins you produce. The meditation that promotes harmony, calm, and balance within you will also penetrate deeply into your womb. Nurturing your body by anointing it with warm oil, and then with strokes of love in self-massage, will contribute to your own sense of body/mind unity. As your baby feels that touch, she'll also receive nurturance. The fuller your self-awareness, the more nurturing you are with yourself and your baby—and the richer the link between mother and fetus, the more joyful the experience of motherhood can be.

The adventure of birthing is a journey, and as with any journey, preparation is required. In this case, preparation and self-nurture are one and the same. Find out what kind of help is available in your area to assist you in birth, what medical techniques are used, and what approaches match your philosophy and personality. Touring various facilities (including those that promote midwifery) can be extremely enlightening. Today, more and more medical doctors espouse natural childbirth and an enhanced and sensitive birthing environment.

You must plan ahead. Ask your mate to join you—for it can make the birth experience all the more meaningful for both of you. Go on as many field trips as necessary to find the environment that feels right. This aspect of discovery is very important. It may seem overwhelming at first, but the more exposure you get to the options available, the easier it will be to make informed choices. One important thing to remember is that you always have the right to change your mind.

I suggest keeping a notebook to log all the questions you'll come up with over time, the experiences your friends and relatives will share with you, and any midwife or doctor referrals that may come your way. Birth is the most significant moment in your newborn's life, and a very important one in your own. The birth environment is something you'll want to plan out well in advance so that you can be calm and confident when your labor starts.

Your Labor and Delivery

For eons, women have given birth naturally. Childbirth is, obviously, an everyday event around the world, and about 95 percent of the time there are no complications. Your hypothalamus and pituitary glands control the hormones in your body, and when the time for birthing comes, your hormones turn on and go into high gear. The understanding that your body knows how to give birth is very comforting—nature even balances the pain of the labor process by providing the pleasure hormone, *oxytocin,* between contractions. Dana McCoy, a certified childbirth educator, describes her experience in this way:

> *After each set of contractions, for two or three minutes I really got a feeling of calm euphoria. I wouldn't say that pain ceased to exist—after all, labor is work. But for me, labor was a different kind of work—it was a mental endeavor to keep myself calm.*
>
> *I accepted what was happening—because when I didn't, my muscles would tense up. As the labor progressed, I felt dreamy and could see colors I don't normally see; it was almost psychedelic. I've heard that oxytocin, which is the main hormone your body releases during childbirth, is actually a hallucinogen if given in large doses. So I felt like I was on a drug without being on a drug.*
>
> *When the baby was born, the pain essentially stopped (or was at least considerably diminished), yet the euphoria continued for hours and hours. It was like a plateau.*

Labor is experienced differently by each of us. Just as no two people are exactly alike, no two women experience labor in the same way. The psychology and mood of the mother-to-be will play an important role in the different levels of intensity and length of labor. Labor is like a unique dance performed by the mother and baby. If either partner resists the flow of the rhythm, the dance will become more painful. The birth force is a powerful rhythm, so flow with it, breathe with it, and dance the dance of birth.

THE CONTRACTIONS BEGIN, AND SOON THEY'LL START TO form a pattern. When the pattern becomes regular, you're entering the first phase of labor. In this phase, the contractions are roughly ten minutes apart. Now you're ready to call your support team—your midwife, your doctor, and anyone you've designated to attend the birth. Your biggest job is to remain cool and focused.

Joy Star, mother of 19-year-old Ayisha, remembers the birth of her daughter as if it were yesterday:

> *I was out dancing the night my water broke. At that time in my life, I had a tendency to get nervous if things didn't go my way. I was still working on my control issues, and they were quite strong. But that night, I didn't get flustered or frustrated, I actually remained calm. Meditation definitely helped me, and it was a wonderful surprise.*
>
> *Ayisha was born five hours later, and I had no pain. It was as if I were caught up in an earthquake and my decision was: "Well, I can either fight it or surrender to it." I realize now that I was both surrendered and committed. It was the best moment in my*

life—I felt exalted in an intuitive way, and it was excellent!

Joy had a beautiful experience because she let her body take over in a very natural way. Yet there are other women who don't know how to surrender and trust their bodies.

Loreli Grace, a lovely and talented artist/business-woman, sent me this emotional story about the birth of her daughter, Sky:

Sky's conception was magical, and my pregnancy was great. I felt so alive and powerful, although I occasionally joked that an alien was growing and taking me over. I refused to read any books on C-section deliveries, even though my mom kept telling me that I'd most likely deliver that way. I wanted to deliver vaginally, like a real "Earth mother." My husband wanted me to have a midwife, and my parents wanted me to deliver in the hospital. Somehow my parents won that argument, and I began to feel less in control. I rationalized to my husband that they just wanted me to be safe. He was disappointed, and I was left alone with my choice.

My contractions started, and I went to the hospital. Soon after I arrived, however, my labor stopped. But I kept having these annoying cramps for many hours, so the next day, my doctor came in and decided to give me a drug to speed up the cramps. The cramps got stronger, and I didn't know what to do. I reacted by tensing up my body, and I kept feeling like I was being assaulted by the cramps. After enduring all day and night like this, I didn't want to feel

anything anymore. So they put a needle in my spine,
laid me on my back, and there was no more pain. I
felt defeated.

The fetus would start to come down, but would
bounce back up. Because my cervix only opened up a
certain amount, the doctor stopped by and decided to
break my water to see if that would help. Meanwhile,
I was getting a fever, and my cervix was exhausted.
My father nodded as my doctor said, "After two days
of labor, we have to do a C-section, now!"

Loreli surrendered, not to her bodily instincts, but to
her doctor and her parents. It's very difficult to change a
preconditioned mind-set. Her mother had delivered
Loreli by C-section and thought it was an inherited condition, but that's rarely the case. In fact, many women
who have experienced C-sections are having vaginal
births with their later children. This is called *V-BAC,* and
presently there's a movement in this country led by
women who are demanding a vaginal delivery after their
C-sections.

Denise McGregor had a C-section with her first baby,
Meghan. She felt detached from the experience of
birthing her own child. She was under anesthesia during
the delivery and didn't get to hold her baby until the
drugs wore off (about four hours later). Her husband
bonded with the baby immediately, whereas she didn't
have that opportunity. She didn't want to repeat that
experience with her second child.

Denise took charge the second time around and
attended a natural childbirth class. She also took a pregnancy yoga class taught by midwives, who suggested that
she have a birthing plan. Denise shared her birthing plan

with her doctor and asked him to consider assisting in a natural birth.

> *I went to my doctor and told him of my birthing plan. I said that I planned on starting my labor at home with a midwife coaching me. But my doctor got defensive and insisted, "You'll have to labor on your back so we can hook a monitor to you."*
>
> *He didn't want a midwife to assist with the birth and also told me that he'd only allow me a certain amount of time to have a natural birth—after that he'd begin a C-section. I guess he wanted to protect himself from a malpractice suit.* [Vaginal deliveries are usually considered high risk if a mother has already had a C-section birth.]
>
> *The midwives recommended other doctors, and the one I chose was fabulous. He worked very actively with the midwives on his team. He was a younger doctor, closer to my age and very much in tune with my birthing philosophy—he didn't have any problems with a V-BAC at all. I had a good intuitive feeling about him, and he answered all of my questions. Although it was the last six weeks of my pregnancy, I called the insurance company and switched doctors. I got all my ducks in a row, and I was sure that everything was being taken care of.*
>
> *My labor began in the afternoon while I was out shopping. At first, my contractions were very erratic. Once home, the time between contractions continued to decrease, but I wasn't dilating. A midwife was at my side, making this a very different labor from my first one. During my first birth, I was sanitized with sheets and gloves and that hospital atmosphere. This*

time I was naked, with my midwife, my friend Shelly, and my husband around me at home.

By midnight, I still was not progressing at all. I screamed, asking for drugs and wanting to go to the hospital. But by the time we got to the hospital, I had dilated from a one to a ten. I frightened the nurse at the front door because I got out of the car and immediately went into a yoga "cat" position on all fours—it was the only comfortable position at the time. I never did get any medication because I was too far along.

Tom called me "The Birth Goddess"—he said I was so incredibly beautiful. The endorphins had an orgasmic quality to them, and I was totally in an altered state. The doctor let me do my own thing—allowing my body to dictate the most comfortable positions to be in. (Western medicine wants you to lie on your back; that means working against gravity and the natural way of your body.) This was so empowering to me because for the first time in my life, I felt in control in an out-of-control situation. I felt power in the middle of surrender . . . it was amazing.

After the birth, I could say to myself: "I have done this! Now I can do anything." I had a strong sense of the connectiveness of my mind and body. Allison came out, and they put her on my chest so that I got to hold her first. It was like she was mine, whereas Meghan had been Tom's, because he'd seen her come out, and I was too drugged to hold her. Allison's birth was so different from the C-section, where I was detached from the experience. Allison's birth was natural—and it's every woman's right to give birth this way.

The process of watching your body transform throughout pregnancy and then finally reaching the pinnacle of creation—the manifestation of a beautiful baby—is as old as time itself, yet uniquely new to each mother. Yes, there is discomfort, uncertainty, and total frustration, but the joy outweighs the pain. The miracle of birth is one of the most profound experiences you'll ever have. It puts your maternal instinct in motion, hones your intuition, and is a rite of passage that forever changes your outlook on life.

So give your delivery time careful consideration before the baby arrives. Decide who you'll want to be there with you (mate, friend, or midwife); under what conditions you'll accept medications for pain or to stimulate contractions; where you want your labor and then the birthing process to be (hospital or home); and how you want to deliver the baby, either vaginally or by C-section. Most important, know your obstetrician's attitudes and philosophy before the birthing process begins.

Many doctors are charming in their office during your prenatal visits but in the delivery room are quite different. Prenatal visits tend to be social encounters, and unless you ask detailed questions about your labor and delivery, you won't be fully prepared for what will happen in the delivery room. Make a list of questions every time you have a prenatal visit—you have a right to know. Don't assume anything: Every doctor has a different view point about midwifery: whether fathers are allowed in the room if a C-section is needed, what position you'll labor in, the use of a birthing chair, and so on. Will you be monitored all through labor, or can it be intermittent so that you can move around? Research the questions, write them down, and don't be afraid to ask your doctor. This will ensure smooth communication, and you'll be more relaxed because you'll know what to expect.

Know yourself, and listen to your inner wisdom when making these monumental decisions. There's no need to fear the natural process of birth. Relax by applying breathing, meditation, and other centering techniques. Trust your body to do what it knows how to do best for you. Know your inner nature, and trust in your body's intelligence.

The Postpartum Period

The time after birth, called *postpartum,* offers a special opportunity to further develop the art of nurturing yourself and your baby. Both mother and baby need nurturing——the mother in order to be prepared for the demands of parenting, and the baby in order to adjust to life outside the womb.

There's much to be said for the miraculous transformation your body goes through during pregnancy; still, once the baby is born, you'll go through another whole transition as hormones change, organs go back into place, and swollen and sore tissues begin to heal. As nature restores your body physically and emotionally, a spiritual transformation may also begin.

I remember when I gave birth for the first time. I was so filled with the wonder of creation that I was moved to tears by just looking at and holding my baby. Many women stay in that wide-open space. It's as if you're between two worlds, and it takes a few days to settle back into your body. There's a heightened awareness of God power, universal power, or spiritual love power—depending on what your cultural or religious background suggests. Remember, *two* births are taking place at this time: the birth of the baby and the birth of you as a mother. Seek the wisdom within yourself, and trust your intuition.

A woman's body dispenses hormones that create the feeling of a natural high at birth and aid in spiritual initiation. The use of anesthesia during childbirth may dull your body's hormonal system for a few days, but when the medication wears off, you'll feel the bountiful bliss of motherhood. Do note, however, that the natural endorphins are blocked not only in the mother, but in the baby as well. Research has proven that babies whose mothers have chosen to have epidural anesthesia have more difficulty finding their mother's breast and nursing immediately after delivery because they've also absorbed the drug, and it disorients them. In a delivery without anesthesia, the natural surge of endorphins that gives mothers that euphoric feeling after childbirth is also received by the child. This makes for a very calm baby. It's your choice to decide which method of birthing is for you. There are pros and cons to both. Talk to other women, learn the differences, and then make an educated decision.

AFTER BIRTH, THERE'S ALSO A NATURAL SECRETION OF HORMONES that gives us the blues, or postpartum depression. I remember plummeting from bliss to despair while still in the hospital. Both my mother and mother-in-law came to see me and couldn't wait to start getting my baby's room filled with baby clothes. I burst out crying, thinking that they were taking away something special that I alone wanted to do. I thought they were intruding. My husband's appearance at my bedside was never long enough or often enough: I cried when he visited me, and I cried when he left. I felt alone even when everyone was around me.

The postpartum period is an emotional one. There are many changes being made during this delicate passage. Your feelings and moods will run the gamut, with an intensity that may surprise you. All of your senses will be exaggerated more than you've ever felt before. One moment you may feel deeply saddened by the emptiness of your womb, and the next you'll be ecstatic as you hold your child in your arms. But all this emotional display is natural. Love yourself enough to allow time and understanding to help you adjust. If this time is held in reverence and respected for the depth of healing it affords, both emotionally and physically, your journey into parenting will be smoother, and your recovery will propel you back to a your pre-pregnant energy state.

Postpartum emotions come in three distinct phases: The first phase is usually referred to as the *postpartum blues*. It can begin about three days after the birth of the baby, and it may last from a few hours to several days. This mood affects up to 89 percent of mothers, and its main symptoms are tearfulness and exhaustion. According to Robin Lim, author of *After the Baby's Birth,* the best way to treat these emotions is to sit down with a dear friend, review the story of your baby's birth, rest, eat well, and cry.

I remember my daughter-in-law, Alisa, telling me that her postpartum blues began the minute she arrived home after giving birth. Although she was in pure joy at the hospital, when she got home, the reality of the overwhelming responsibility hit her.

*I started crying when I realized that I'd have my
two dogs and three cats to contend with, and all of my*

family coming over before I was able to adjust to motherhood—it just overwhelmed me. I could have cried at the drop of a pin.

The day Marc went back to work, I was upset that he was leaving me alone with the baby. Even though I had baby-sat a great deal as a teenager and had assisted my mother with my sister (16 years my junior), I was panicked at the thought of being alone with the baby. I felt isolated.

Most new mothers experience some feelings of helplessness and doubt, like Alisa did. But the second phase, called *moderate postpartum depression,* affects only about 10 to 20 percent of new mothers. It can begin 2 weeks to 18 months after delivery, and can last up to a year. It's marked by one, all, or a combination of the following: sleeplessness, self-doubt, fears, loss of interest in sex, frequent crying, or emotional numbness. To remedy this imbalance, seek loving support from family and friends, get professional advice and/or guidance (including sound advice from doctors regarding medications if needed), examine your diet (see the nutritional suggestions for postpartum tonics later in this chapter), balance your dosha, take walks, and do something nice for yourself every day. Make time to luxuriate in a bubble bath, and review the centering techniques suggested in Chapter 3.

The third phase of postpartum depression, also called *puerperal psychosis,* is severe and affects less than 3 percent of new mothers. It's a total breakdown of the ability to cope, and may include some of the moderate postpartum symptoms. If you fear you may injure your baby or yourself, or if you experience violent outbursts, blackouts, or loss of memory, *immediately seek experienced professional help.* You and your baby could be in danger. Prescribed medications and/or hormonal therapy (including progesterone) are proven and effective treatments for this condition. Remember, unconditional love and solid support systems are always beneficial, and with this type of depression, they're essential.

It's interesting to learn from other cultures and their unique approaches to the postpartum period. Around the world, women sing the blues after giving birth. In her book *Mamatoto,* a collection of cultural practices celebrating the wonder of birth throughout the world, author Carroll Dunham describes a traditional Malaysian treatment for women who have the "baby blues." First, they're helped blessed and anointed using incantations and water that has been put through a special magic treatment. "If that doesn't work," Dunham writes, "a spirit-raising seance is held. The mother, in a trance state, is encouraged to express all her negative emotions, her angers, her fears, and anxieties, her ambivalent feelings about being a mother."[1]

Take encouragement from the fact that postpartum depression is recognized by cultures new and old around the world. Know that you aren't making it up, and consider allowing yourself a kind of ceremonial release, by talking out your fears, anxieties, and emotions, with a support group of family and/or friends. If that isn't possible, write down your feelings. When you've seen your anxieties and fears on paper, many of them will be dispelled. Music is also a great healer, so turn up your favorite tunes. In Chapter 3, I mentioned Gandharva-Veda music—compositions that mirror the changing rhythms in nature. You might find this especially calming.

Ayurveda also suggests flute music because it's very sooth-ing to babies and mothers alike.

Of course, lack of time is probably the number-one complaint of new mothers throughout the world as they struggle to adjust to schedules and new energy levels. One solution to this problem of time management that's used more commonly in other cultures is inviting relatives and friends who are eager to visit you to help you with your daily tasks. A little help with your other kids, meals, housework, errands, and laundry can be just what you need. In family-centered communities, such as Maui, Hawaii, mothers are working to improve their postpartum experiences. By networking, friends bring food and vol-unteer to do housecleaning. Mothers, babies, and entire families gather to share experiences, enjoy potluck meals, and watch films. Through these experiences, friendships grow that last a lifetime.

Bonding with Your Baby After Birth

The bond you established with your baby when she was inside you will continue to blossom if you both stay balanced. A postpartum program of wellness inspired by Ayurveda will help your baby sense your healthy recov-ery and feel your grounded centeredness and bliss. Meditation, yoga positions, and abhyanga (oil massage) are three basic practices you shouldn't leave behind after your baby's birth. You need to include them in your daily routine as preventive measures to ensure your health. Remember that your baby has special needs at this time, too. She'll be adjusting to a world of sights, sounds, and smells different from the world of the womb she occupied for nine months.

You may not be used to sharing yourself with some-one so much. Babies do need constant care, but *all* the care doesn't have to come from you. Today, father's are wonderful helpers. In fact, Ayurveda encourages fathers to sleep near the baby and share in the care. That way, when your baby stirs during the night, a gentle pat can reassure her of her parents' presence and affection. Fathers haven't carried the baby for nine months, so they don't have the natural instincts that mothers have, but they can learn to be more aware of their baby's needs by taking care of him or her. Once a father bonds with his child, his awareness will increase.

Ayurveda holds that breast-feeding is best for the child and for the mother. Being in the moment when you breast-feed allows you to experience the joy of watching your baby suckle. Pay attention to the baby during feed-ing; don't watch TV or discuss serious affairs with your husband or partner. Just enjoy this natural wonder. My own experience of breast-feeding taught me that the best nursing experiences and the most successful feedings took place when no one else was around and there weren't any distractions. It's a sacred time for you and your baby, so enjoy it—it can never be replaced. The time you spend with your baby now will set the foundation for parenting.

Dani Newman, the Navy nurse we met in Chapter 1, realized after a trip abroad how much she missed by not having a long postpartum recovery and bonding time with her baby.

When my little girl, Jamie, was three years old,
I took her to Finland—where I'd lived in my teens.

My teenage friends were now in their 40s and had children. In Finland, mothers get 11 months off work to care for their babies, so when my friends heard I went back to work 8 weeks after delivering Jamie, they were horrified. They said, "How could anyone but the mother care for the baby?" It was then that I then recognized how wounded I was by our society.

One of my friends is an architect and engineer—a very liberated woman—yet she was staying at home and nursing her baby. I felt envy and sadness that I didn't have that experience. Finland supports women . . . and motherhood.

Dani felt cheated out of the time she spent at work instead of with her baby. She realized that Western society makes women feel guilty if they choose to stay home with their new babies to bond and care for them. Dani went back to work because she was worried about losing her job.

That was six years ago. Today, more women are taking a stand to stay home longer—and some businesses are honoring extended maternity leave as a business perk. The Family and Medical Leave Act of 1996 covers the private sector of employers who have 50 or more employees as well as some governmental employees. Under FMLA, employers must grant 12 weeks of unpaid leave in a calendar year to parents of a newborn, of a newly adopted child, or of a sick child. This is an improvement, and more help is on its way through proposed amendments to this bill extending and expanding the coverage. Our society needs to take a look at how we honor women, birth, and the postpartum period, and make changes so that mothers who choose to care for their babies at home get the support they need.

Alisa, my daughter-in-law, explains how she felt conflicted over her desire to stay home with her baby and the pressure from society for women to return to work:

> *Around the third through sixth months, I started feeling jealous of my husband's work at law school and his law-clerking job. I'd ask myself where my future was going—it seemed that the daily routine was doing me in. I'd cringe when people asked me what I did, because nowadays, staying home to raise your baby is looked at as not enough. Self-doubt became an on-and-off-again emotion, and at night I'd cry. I knew I was blessed not to have to go back to work, and my baby, Shelby, was thriving because of the bonding and joy we shared daily. But society's dim view of "just staying home" continued to haunt me for a few months.*

The Ayurvedic Postpartum Prescription

This 5,000-year-old tradition offers some useful hints to help you and your baby through the postpartum period.

REST

The six-week period after the birth of a baby can be exhausting. You'll probably feel drained at times—the chores and responsibilities that come with having a new baby can seem enormous. But if you take the time for practices that nurture and restore you, you may feel even better than you did before you got pregnant. Even interrupted sleep can be turned into a time for insight: Remember your dreams and contemplating their meanings; write or tape-record your birth story for your new child and for yourself. Include your mate's memory of the birth in your story, as this can provide a real catharsis for both of you.

The postpartum period involves a transition on physical, mental, and emotional levels. In our society, we have a real tendency to rush the recovery period because we feel we have to multitask, go back to work, and fulfill other obligations. But in the Indian tradition of Ayurveda, the first 22 days after delivery (at least) are dedicated to pampering the new mother. The Maharishi Ayur-Veda Center's Mother/Baby Program advocates extending this period to 40 days. During this period of rest, few (if any) visitors are allowed during this time so that the mother and baby can get the rest they need. Mothers and children are also encouraged to stay out of wind and weather in order to decrease exposure to disease.

Just as you must listen when your instincts alert you to your new baby's discomforts, you must also listen when it comes to your own body's cries for care. Know when you need rest, and go back to bed. Sleep when your baby sleeps—otherwise you'll constantly be tired. Take the baby with you, and snuggle together while you nap. Mothers and babies need closeness—after all, you've been together for nine months. This is a healthy and natural part of parenting.

MASSAGE

Another wonderful Ayurvedic treatment to take advantage of is massage. Have a massage technician come to your home and give you a massage every day for six weeks. Not only is massage therapeutic, and good for circulation and muscle tension, but it also helps promote relaxation in painful areas. After the massage, take a hot bath. This nurturing time is very important because it gives you time for yourself. If you're unable to have a massage every day, take an hour and a half when you can, and make it your special respite.

A specialized technician isn't the only one who can provide this valuable service: Perhaps your partner can give you a loving massage. Massage is a way of giving pleasure, so who better to give the massage than your mate? Touching is a two-way stimulation that can benefit your relationship as well as improve your general health.

In India, the midwife or grandmother will massage the baby for the first few weeks. When the mother regains her strength, she'll take over the loving ritual of massage. (See Chapter 4 for detailed information about baby massage.)

TONICS

Ayurveda recommends that new mothers drink two servings daily of the following tonic to stimulate healthy breast milk: To two cups of boiled milk, add ⅛ teaspoon ginger, ⅛ teaspoon cardamom, and a pinch of saffron. Add brown sugar and ghee to taste if desired. Ghee relaxes Vata, agrees with Pitta, but should be avoided by Kapha.

To turn this into a light and pleasant rice dish, add the milk tonic to two to three cups cooked brown rice (one cup dry) together with salt, turmeric, coriander, and cumin to taste. (Almonds are also a good snack food for promoting healthy breast milk—just make sure the almonds are blanched for easier digestion.)

Ayurveda favors simple meals during the postpartum passage. A basic dahl (legume dish) of red lentils cooked in water with ghee and curry powder is an easy to prepare and very nourishing postpartum food. A staple in India, basmati rice is also highly recommended during the postpartum period because it's easy to digest and strengthens the body. Coconut is soothing for mothers with postpartum blues; it also calms Pitta and is good for PMS.

Postpartum digestion may be somewhat out of balance, causing new moms to experience gas as well as constipation. To reduce discomfort, add one teaspoon whole fennel seeds to two quarts of water, and boil for up to ten minutes. Let cool until warm, and drink the tea throughout the day. A little fresh lemon juice squeezed onto main dishes also aids digestion.

Vata disorders such as constipation, depression, and gas are very common during the postpartum period. You can avoid such imbalances by following a Vata-balancing diet. (This diet is recommended for all doshas at this time, and can be found in Chapter 6).

Taking proper care of your body will help you recover faster and allow nature to restore and balance your bodily functions. It's crucial at this time to pay attention to your physical needs—in the long run, it will give you the strength you need to be the best parent you can be.

Adjusting to Motherhood—Honoring Yourself and Your Relationships

At this new time in your life, you're gifted with *pure potentiality*. However, no matter how high your intentions to be a good parent are, if you don't take the time to recuperate, parenthood can become burdensome and your spousal relationship may bear much of this stress. This is a vulnerable time for mother, baby, and your relationship with a partner, so everyone in your family will need to make adjustments.

Before the baby comes, design a secure emotional "nest"—a place that's special and private to you and your partner. It may be your own bed, where you can relax and share intimate memories of your life together and feelings for each other, or it can be a romantic lovers' lane away from your home. Create a romantic ritual that allows you both a retreat as well as the opportunity to renew and reinforce your love for each other. Consider giving each other gifts that represent your life together, and your new life once the baby comes—they can be as simple as mementos found in nature or inspirational poems.

Start observing your romantic ritual with your partner as soon as possible after the birth, and continue to do so on a regular basis. Remember that this is your time together, and it must be your own time exclusive of others (including the baby). Even if it's only 30 minutes every Sunday evening, don't underestimate the value and the power of your romantic time to strengthen your bond and enhance the intimacy between the two of you.

Another way to foster that intimacy is by making a concerted effort to include your partner in parenting. Don't exclude your partner from interacting with you when you tend the baby. Make your mate feel special with a gesture of love in the presence of the baby. Lie in your bed with your mate, and play with your new baby and share the delight. Snuggle with your mate while cradling the baby. You have something new to share together; don't push your mate away because you feel more competent as a caregiver.

Don't forget to use your knowledge of your mind/body type to your advantage. Ayurveda can help you focus on your special needs at this time based on your dosha and its dominant characteristics. For example, a Vata-type person may need to slow down and stop doing so many things at once, and a Kapha-type person may be in for a jolt because the demands of a baby can push her into more activity than she's used to. Remember the three keys to your recovery—rest, massage, and tonics. Especially in the first six weeks, these three things will help you regain your strength.

As the demands of motherhood unfold, don't be shy about asking for an hour of help from a friend, a neighbor, or a relative; you may even consider hiring help. The most important thing is to make sure that this helper will nurture you so that you can nurture your baby. I remember my sweet mother-in-law's generous offer to hire a nurse to help me in the first few weeks after delivery. The nurse was a family friend who had assisted my sisters-in-law when her children were born.

The nurse, Collie, was a dear older woman with one—and only one—purpose as far as she was concerned: to take care of the baby. She never allowed me to hold the baby except when I was nursing. She dressed, bathed, and comforted the baby—and she got angry when I interfered with her routine. It was a nightmare.

Being young and inexperienced, I listened to my husband, who said his mother knew best. Even my own mother stepped back, intimidated by the professional nurse who had been assigned the task of getting my baby, Marc, on a good schedule.

Every mother wants to focus on her newborn—how she's eating, breathing, eliminating, and sleeping. Because it's all new, it may feel overwhelming at times. Yet most mothers wouldn't want it to be any other way. I've learned over the years that my maternal instincts were perfectly fine: I should have been the one to care for my baby. Collie would have served a much better purpose had she nurtured *me*. I would have welcomed a daily massage to decrease my body's soreness, stiffness, and lingering puffiness. And I could have learned some valuable tips about baby care had the nurse been willing to share her knowledge and experience with me.

Women can learn to nurture themselves and to allow others to nurture them as well, perhaps even developing communities of women who support and lend help during the postpartum period. Networking in this way helps us develop friendships that will grow with us throughout our lives, and hopefully we'll begin a tradition that will serve as a legacy to our daughters.

It's my hope that there will be a paradigm shift in the collective thinking of pregnant women so that self-awareness will inspire the continued use and acceptance of Ayurveda, the remarkable 5,000-year-old system for preventive health. Every woman wants her child to live life fully and completely—Ayurveda shows the way to maintaining your baby's natural balance and to restoring your own. The theme of balance that's the hallmark of Ayurveda and the central idea of this book must now be put into practice by integrating each secret into your daily life and reinforcing them at every opportunity.

It's my wish to demonstrate through instruction and practice the seven secrets to health and happiness for you and your child: caring for yourself and your child even before conception, learning about doshas, meditating and centering, massage, yoga, nutrition, and nurturing. Find the best approach to ensure health for you and your baby. The mind/body concept will then become a natural way of life.

It's my dream that the journey of life for each new baby begins in a happy, secure, healthful environment. A blissful childhood depends on a centered, balanced, and loving family. Only in this way can we cultivate happy and healthy children and allow them to retain the blissful feelings of love they come to us with.

Summary

+ Nurturing yourself when you're pregnant gives you a fuller awareness of your body and mind, resulting in a more meaningful birth experience.

+ Prepare for the journey of birth by keeping a notebook with all the questions you have and getting them answered.

+ A woman who knows her body already knows how to give birth—it's not a conscious thought process.

+ Giving birth can be the best moment in your life if you surrender to it, so don't fight it—commit to it.

+ Staying in a balanced, healthful state after birth will help you and your baby remain bonded and continue to grow closer.

+ It's important to include your partner in parenting and to make a special time alone together to renew and reinforce your relationship.

+ Ayurvedic practices and techniques can ease the postpartum period and get mother back to her pre-pregnancy state of balance.

+++   +++

✦ ✦ ✦ ✦ ✦ ✦ ✦

EPILOGUE

✦ ✦ ✦ ✦ ✦ ✦ ✦

The fibers of each of the seven secrets in this book were woven together with love. Love is the only thing that can ensure that each secret in this book is executed with heartfelt care. The love I feel for my own children, my grandchild, and every child on the planet has maintained my interest throughout my life and held my focus for the last several years, during which time I completed this book.

Throughout the writing of *Seven Secrets to Raising a Happy and Healthy Child,* I was reminded of my own children's early years . . . and how I wish I'd had these valuable mind/body secrets to utilize throughout their development. Yet in retrospect, I gave them the greatest mind/body secret of all—*unconditional love,* which I believe is nature's highest emotion. Just as my mother enveloped me with her unconditional love, so did I with my children. I followed my own maternal instinct and used it as my ultimate guide. Trust in your own intuition. So many times we think that someone else will know better how to fix our problems, but inside each of us is the perfect answer to most questions.

By learning and utilizing the dosha profiles of yourself and your child, you'll be better able to answer simple health questions before running to the doctor. Understanding the doshas helps us adjust the environment to best suit our child's needs. (Of course, if any problem persists, by all means see your physician.)

My granddaughter, Shelby (now approaching her third birthday), is a bubbly, vibrant child with all the panache of a Vata. Her creative approach to life is encouraged by her parents, who take her everywhere, read to her daily, massage her frequently, and find time to honor silence with her. She doesn't have a baby brother or sister as of yet, but when she does, I'm confident that the mind/body practices delicately instituted with Shelby will be even easier to establish with the second baby. Practice makes perfect.

Raising a child is the most challenging, frustrating, and exhausting job you'll ever have—and yet it's the most exhilarating, beautiful, and rewarding accomplishment you'll ever achieve. Parenthood brings with it a joy that can carry you throughout your life. In these mega-electronic, digital, laser, and cyber times, we need to go back to fundamental values and practices that ensure preventive health and stability in the challenging times ahead.

Love is what we need in order to put all of these elements into motion so they won't be "secrets" any longer. Ultimately, the results will certainly be happy and healthy children who can accept the changes around them and see the gifts in all of life.

+++ +++

+ + + + +

NOTES

+ + + + +

Introduction

1. Nancy Lonsdorf, M.D., Veronica Butler, M.D., and Melanie Brown, Ph.D., *A Woman's Best Medicine: Health, Happiness, and Long Life through Ayur-Veda* (G.P. Putnam's Sons, Inc., New York, 1993), 8.

Chapter 1

1. Nancy Lonsdorf, et. al., 248.
2. Jennifer Louden, *The Pregnant Woman's Comfort Book: A Self-Nurturing Guide to Your Emotional Well-Being During Pregnancy and Early Motherhood* (Harper San Francisco, San Francisco, 1995), 18.

Chapter 2

1. Nancy Lonsdorf, et. al., 59.
2. Deepak Chopra, M.D., *Perfect Health: The Complete Mind Body Guide* (Harmony Books, New York, 1991), 304.
3. Chopra, p. 303.

Chapter 3

1. Deepak Chopra, M.D., *Ageless Body, Timeless Mind: The Quantum Alternative to Growing Old* (Harmony Books, New York, 1993), 163.
2. Inayat Khan, *Education: From before Birth to Maturity* (Hunter House, Claremont, CA, 1989), 112.
3. Robert Tisserand, *The Essential Oil Safety Data Manual* (Tisserand Aroma-therapy Institute, Sussex, England, 1988).

Chapter 4
1. Vimala Schneider, *Infant Massage: A Handbook for Loving Parents* (New York: Bantam Books, 1989), 133.

Chapter 5
1. Georg Feuerstein and Stephan Bodian with the staff of *Yoga Journal,* eds., *Living and Yoga: A Comprehensive Guide for Daily Life.* (New York: G. P. Putnam's Sons, Inc., 1993), 2.
2. Yoga International, *Balancing Active and Receptive Energies: The Practice of Nadi Shodhanam* (Honesdale, PA: Himalayan Institute Press, 1993), 2.

Chapter 6
1. Dr. Robert E. Svoboda, *Prakruti: Your Ayurvedic Constitution* (Albequerque, NM: Geocom Limited, 1989), 58.
2. Kathleen Huggins, R.N.M.S. *The Nursing Mother's Companion* (Boston, MA: Harvard Common Press, 1995), 3.

Chapter 7
1. Carroll Dunham and the Body Shop Team, *Mamatoto: A Celebration of Birth* (New York: Penguin Books, 1991), 126.

✦✦✦   ✦✦✦

ABOUT THE AUTHOR

Joyce Golden Seyburn's love for children has been the central theme in her life. She received a B.S. in education from Wayne State University and proceeded to teach kindergarten and first grade. While her three children were young, she worked on her master's degree in early childhood development and also wrote articles for *The Detroit News* and various magazines.

After volunteering at the Center for Mind/Body Medicine, Deepak Chopra's first West Coast well-being center, she found out that she was soon to become a grandmother for the first time. Searching for mind/body parenting books to share with her children and finding none, she decided to write her own. She then began *Seven Secrets to Raising a Happy and Healthy Child,* the first book on the Ayurvedic approach to parenting. Currently, she speaks on mind/body issues for parents.

+++   +++

NOTES

NOTES

NOTES

✦✦✦

We hope you enjoyed this Hay House book.
If you would like to receive a free catalog featuring
additional Hay House books and products,
or if you would like information about the
Hay Foundation, please contact:

Hay House, Inc.
P.O. Box 5100
Carlsbad, CA 92018-5100

(760) 431-7695 or (800) 654-5126
(760) 431-6948 (fax) or (800) 650-5115 (fax)
www.hayhouse.com

✦✦✦

Published and distributed in Australia by:
Hay House Australia Pty Ltd, 18/36 Ralph St.,
Alexandria NSW 2015 • *Phone:* 612-9669-4299
Fax: 612-9669-4144 • *E-mail:* info@hayhouse.com.au

Published and Distributed in the United Kingdom by:
Hay House UK, Ltd. • Unit 202, Canalot Studios •
222 Kensal Rd., London W10 5BN
Phone: 020-8962-1230 • *Fax:* 020-8962-1239

Distributed in Canada by:
Raincoast • 9050 Shaughnessy St., Vancouver, B.C. V6P 6E5
Phone: (604) 323-7100 • *Fax:* (604) 323-2600

✦✦✦